PASSPORT TO EUROPE

PICTURES AND STORIES FROM QUEEN OF THE SOUTH'S INCREDIBLE CUP-RUN 2007-08

KENNY RAMSAY

Published in association with
QUEEN OF THE SOUTH FC

JAM
BOOK PUBLISHING

PASSPORT TO EUROPE

First edition published in 2008 by **JAM BOOK PUBLISHING**

in association with Queen of the South Football Club

Text & Design © **JAM BOOK PUBLISHING** 2008

Art Direction & Design: Jim Lockwood

Picture Editing: Matthew Ashton

Foreword & Introduction: Robert Grieve

Sub-editor: Bruce Wright

Match stats: Ian Black

Additional pictures: Duncan Brown (Peterhead); David Henderson and
Andrew West (Linlithgow Rose); Willie Vass (semi-final and final)

All written material forms the opinions of the contributing writers and are
not necessarily those of the publisher or Queen of the South Football Club.

For all queries concerning this publication please write to:

JAM BOOK PUBLISHING

PO Box 979, Shrewsbury, UK, SY3 7XB

info@jambookpublishing.com

www.jambookpublishing.com

Printed in China 2008

22 49 56 60 12 04 08

A CIP catalogue for this book is
available from the British Library

ISBN 978-0-9556518-2-3

ACKNOWLEDGEMENTS

To the following contributors of stories and anecdotes: Donald Adamson; Walt Adamson; David Balmanno; Ian Black;
Callum Blackley; Robin Blanefield; Paul Burns; Ken Carlaw; Scot Carrick; Gordon Chisholm; Kate Clark; Liam Cullen;
Iain Dalling; Simon Davidson; Steve Davies; Colin Faulds; Eric Fisher; Ross Fraser; Harley Freemantle; Jock Gardiner; Bill
Goldie; Ron and Lindy Gottlieb; Alan Hall; Lindsay Hanson; Jim Harkness; Gordon Harper; Craig Hodgson; James Hogg;
Stuart Holden; Rachel Irving; John Ivison; Philip Jackson; Stephen Jardine; William Johnstone; Simon Jowitt; Scott Kerr;
John Kerr; Derek and Fiona Kirkpatrick; Peter Latchford; Geoff Leonard; Ewan Lithgow; Fraser MacLean; Martin McGarva
Smith; Chris McKie; Mark McMinn; Andy Meaden; Graham Mills; Jennifer Moffat; Les Morton; Paul Nelson; Sean O'Connor;
Mark Ovens; Andy Paterson; Craig Paterson; Andrew Penn; Robbie Purdie; David Rae; Gordon Rae; Stuart Rae; Rob
Richardson; John Rodgers; Chris Saunderson; Kenny Scott; Mark Seaton; Ian Spence; John Stewart; Murray Sutherland;
Ineke Thomson; Jim Thomson; Bruce Wright; Iain Wright; Joanna Wright; Tommy Young.

Thanks to Scottish Sun editor David Dinsmore for backing me and as always to picture editor Mark Sweeney.

Special thanks to Bruce Wright for all his work and support, the Queens' supporters' club secretaries for spreading the
word, Footymad website host Eric Fisher who helped to promote the book and the pictures and to the Chairman, Directors
and staff of Queen of the South FC for their support with this publication.

Additional thanks to Gordon Chisholm, Kenny Brannigan and the players for putting up with me during the cup run,
particularly during the pre-cup final break. It was magic.

Finally, to my wife Janette for agreeing to take the gamble and my children Katie, Heather and Paul, I love you all.

PASSPORT TO EUROPE

PICTURES AND STORIES FROM QUEEN OF THE SOUTH'S INCREDIBLE CUP-RUN 2007-08

KENNY RAMSAY

CONTENTS

FOREWORD
DAVID RAE

August 22, 1948. That was the day I saw my very first game of football. I was 11 years of age and it was a match between Queen of the South and Partick Thistle at Palmerston. Queens won 8-2. Billy Houliston, who played three times for Scotland, scored five goals. I walked four miles to get the bus and did the same journey on the way home again. My mother and father thought I would be dead tired but I burst through the front door jumping three feet high because of what I'd just seen with my own eyes.

It seems like a long, long time ago now, having that feeling of excitement. Maybe because it is. But from that day 'til this, there has only ever been one team for me. That's what makes the Scottish Cup run of 2007/08 all the more remarkable. Sixty years passed in between times but the feeling of joy I had at Hampden on May 24, 2008 was better than ever.

People throughout the years have often asked me which club I support and when I say Queens they say: 'yeah, but which OTHER team.' 'I'm sorry,' I'll tell them, 'but there is only one team for me.' I've supported the club through thick and thin and never thought I'd ever see them in

a Scottish Cup final. That's why it's quite simply the greatest achievement in the history of Queen of the South football club. There is no doubt about that.

The club reached the semi-final half a century ago but since then there hasn't been anything close. The run itself was exhilarating each and every step of the way. For various reasons each tie had its own excitement from where it all began against Peterhead, to the junior opposition in Linlithgow Rose.

We faced Dundee, still a huge club in the First Division, before Aberdeen who are maybe in the top five in the whole of the country. We didn't expect to be playing them in the semi-final given they were up against Celtic in the quarter-finals but they pulled off a magnificent result in a replay.

But for me our Scottish Cup semi-final with Aberdeen will go down in history as the best ever. That was certainly the media reaction to the game and I firmly go along with that. Particularly the second half, it went from end to end as though no one was stopping to draw breath. The pace of the game was amazing with open football played by ➡

'David Rae is Queens through and through and is always worried about what the fans think. He is a supporters' Chairman'

Jim Thomson, Captain, Queen of the South FC

both sides. For us to win that game by a scoreline of 4-3 speaks volumes for the character of our side. My abiding memory of that afternoon was when Aberdeen hit the crossbar and the upright. Once that happened I turned to my fellow directors, clenched my fists and said: 'you know something, this is going to be our day.' I just felt when that happened that Aberdeen weren't going to be able to beat us. Overall we deserved to win that match because no matter how many times Aberdeen equalised we refused to let our heads go down and actually got stronger.

I just think it's so marvellous, and fitting, that the team wrote its name into the club's history books with such an amazing performance in such a thrilling match. Personally reaching the final was most certainly the greatest moment in my time as chairman of Queen of the South.

It would have been something extra special to go on and lift the trophy itself but we were up against Rangers. They walked off the pitch at the end of the match knowing they'd been in a game and that says everything as far as I'm concerned. For 20 minutes of that second half they were rocking. I've heard it said that our boys sat back a

little bit after they scored the second goal but I'm not so sure that's the case. I just think they took so much out of themselves that we were maybe just drained.

The fact that we hadn't had a competitive game for four weeks before the final maybe had something to do with that. Even training as hard as we did, it maybe helped swing the balance ever so slightly in Rangers' favour. I think people should just bear in mind that up until that point Queen of the South had only spent £10,000 on playing talent. I haven't ever sat down and counted how much the Rangers team cost but I'd guess it was a little more than that. In fact, I'd reckon it's a figure closer to £20million!

That's what makes it such a phenomenal achievement just reaching the final. Now that I've had a taste of an occasion like that, I wouldn't mind going back.

I must be honest, though, and say I don't expect I'll see it happen again. With this club though and a manager like Gordon Chisholm and his backroom staff, who knows...

David Rae,
Chairman, Queen of the South

INTRODUCTION
GORDON CHISHOLM

The look on my face probably says it all. That's maybe just as well, because I don't think I'll ever have the words to describe what it was like. Not the feeling I had deep inside as I walked up the steps at Hampden at the end of one unforgettable Scottish Cup campaign.

There was extreme frustration. There was bitter disappointment. More than that, though, enormous pride. In what we'd done. How far we'd gone. A journey none us of ever imagined possible way back at the beginning. Yet there's that lingering taste still stuck at the back of my throat telling me it could have been so much better.

The first game was against Peterhead and people said that was a potential banana skin for us. We were expected to slip up. We didn't and won by five. Then we were up against junior opposition and again everyone expected us to fall flat on our faces. Stevie Tosh made sure of that when he said the reason junior clubs were junior was because they weren't good enough and we'd batter them. And we did. Every game was like that in some way. Dundee were sitting above us in the league but we managed to win again, the boy McCann scoring from 84 yards – outrageous. There was just no stopping us.

When Aberdeen beat Celtic 1-0 at Parkhead I went away from the stadium thinking to myself: 'we could go all the way, you know.' That's how you start to think when you're so close to a Scottish Cup final. Aberdeen were standing in our way but by that point I didn't fear anyone. No one at the club did. Aberdeen had us watched against Stirling and Livingston and we were without big O'Connor. He was sitting in the stand, injured, and I remember thinking it could turn out to be a blessing. We were a totally different side when he played and I got it into my head Aberdeen didn't know what to expect. I genuinely believed we might just catch them by surprise.

The semi-final itself was a game I don't think will ever be bettered. I've certainly never witnessed anything like it. Scottish Cup semi-finals aren't meant to be like that. Our boys just never stopped from start to finish. Managers talk about belief and we had it that day. It's funny, I remember Stevie Tosh actually asking Jamie MacDonald to check when his contract ran out. This was in the dressing room minutes before we played Aberdeen and after thinking about it Jamie suddenly realised his deal expired before the cup final. All of a sudden all the boys were ➡

> '**The gaffer is the best I have worked with. The training is brilliant, he is an excellent man manager and he helps create a good atmosphere at the club which you just want to be part of**'
>
> Sean O'Connor, Queen of the South FC

asking about their contracts and what would happen. That shows the kind of belief we had, the moment the game started the boys were immense. Each time Aberdeen pegged us back our boys raised their game again and kept going. Alright, we carried a bit of luck when they hit the bar but you need that on these types of occasions. We deserved everything we got that day.

Not that I was any use. At one point I ran down to the side of the pitch and shouted over wee Burnsy and told him: 'just sit in tight and make it a midfield four.' By the time I turned around he was over on the other side at out-side left! I just turned around to the boys beside me and said: 'I'm wasting my time going down there.' It was just one of those games which had to run its course. You can try and change things – do something tactically – but the truth of the matter is that the boys were just out there playing. The problem after that was that four weeks was a long time to wait for the final. I know it sounds like an excuse but my honest opinion is that I don't think it was fair.

There was an element of stage fright, I'm not denying that. Rangers didn't play us in that first half. I don't know who it was they were up against but it wasn't the boys I recognised. That's

all I said to them at half-time. 'There are 17,000 Queens fans out there, you're live on TV and you perform like that!' I wasn't having it and thankfully neither were they. What a turnaround. They grabbed the game by the scruff of the neck and managed to get it back to 2-2.

I just wish we could have kept it tight after that and then taken the game to extra time, but it wasn't to be. We'd reached a stage where things just didn't go for us.

It's funny because we watched Rangers against Aberdeen on the Thursday before the final and left with five minutes to go. As we got to the car we heard Rangers had a man sent off. 'Please let it be Nacho Novo,' I heard myself saying, and it was. He was someone I was worried about because of his pace and his red card ruled him out of the cup final. It was another indication that things might just go our way. Ah well...

Walking up those steps afterwards was a hard task, I'll not lie, purely because I knew we could have won it, should have won it. But any frustration I had then or still have now is overtaken by something else altogether, and that's pride. Nothing will ever take that away.

Gordon Chisholm
Manager, Queen of the South

CHAPTER 1
PETERHEAD

We gave Peter a sair heid

PETERHEAD 0, QUEEN OF THE SOUTH 5

SATURDAY 24 NOVEMBER 2007

SCOTTISH CUP 3RD ROUND

Balmoor Stadium

QUEENS SCORERS: **Dobbie 27, 89, O'Connor 44, 57, Burns 90**

Attendance: **695**

QUEEN OF THE SOUTH

1	MacDonald
2	Paton
3	Harris
4	Aitken
5	Thomson
6	Gilmour (**14** Robertson, 88)
7	Burns
8	Tosh
9	Scally
10	O'Connor (**13** O'Neill, 85)
11	Dobbie

SUBS NOT USED:

12	Grindlay
15	MacFarlane
16	McQuilken

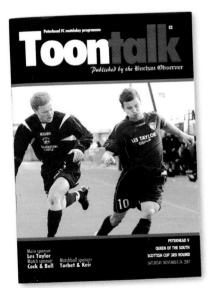

For a change we left the house for a Queens away game at 2.15pm – reason we stay in Peterhead – we must have been the only two Queens fans that were happy when we drew the Bluetooners

Derek and Fiona Kirkpatrick
Peterhead

24 November 2007 and the Doonhamers Travel Club bus picks me up in Dunblane en route to Peterhead and the start of the 2007/08 Scottish Cup adventure.

Its 08.15 and the bus has already been on the road for almost 2 hours – these are dedicated people. I feel a bit guilty that I was in my bed half an hour ago. Despite being alone (Dunblane is not a hotbed of QOS fans) and unknown to anyone on the bus I am warmly welcomed and the journey passes quickly.

Upon arrival at Balmoor we are welcomed into the social club (pre-arranged I think) and I am adopted by Musky and Jimmydoubt (+ Jimmydoubt junior). The conversation is easy and enjoyable and it turns out my mother once worked with Jimmydoubt's mother – it is indeed a small world.

By kick-off time we are well watered and fed and really looking forward to the game. The 5-0 victory maintains everybody's good spirits despite the fact that Peterhead is even colder than legend would have it. The funniest chant of the day is directed at some who head for the warmth of the bus before the game is finished – "We can see you, we can see you, we can see you keeping warm, we can see you keeping warm".

The bus leaves and Luke11's quiz proves too tough for any chance to impress anybody although some of the questions are a bit obscure. Before I know it we are in Auchterarder and we stop for a comfort break. I am leaving the pub when I hear someone from the other bus (there are two buses) call my name. It's a guy from the year above me at Dumfries Academy who I remember well and we talk about the intervening 36 years since we were at school together. Is it really 36 years since the 1970/71 Dumfries Academy 1st XI all dreamed about playing for The Mighty South?

Back on the road and it's only 15 miles to Dunblane where I get dropped off. It's almost 22.00 as I head for the pub to bore people who have never heard of QOS with tales of Yer Hame Team's Yer Ain Team. (Fast forward to 24 May 2008 – they've all heard of them now!!!!!)

The bus will be on the road for another 2 hours – these are dedicated people. I feel a bit guilty that I will be in my bed in half an hour.

Les Morton,
Dunblane

I'm one of the lucky hundred or so who made it to all six Scottish Cup games. Although that was down to luck as much as anything. I'd provisionally arranged to pick up some Christmas presents from my dad and aunt who both live near Aberdeen on the weekend of the 24th November. When we drew Peterhead there was no contest.

I'd never been to Balmoor before and it was absolutely bitter with a cold wind blowing off the North Sea. I'd my duvet jacket on but hadn't time for even a quick beer before kick off. About half-time and with Queens two up, some of the less hardy Queens fans realised that the Travel Club bus was parked behind the goal at the seaward end and the windows were higher than the wall. Realising it would be less Arctic, a dozen or so fans went and watched the rest of the game from the bus! Cue a new song from those fans still braving the elements behind the goal – "We can see you, we can see you, we can see you keeping warm, we can see you keeping warm!" Just to reinforce the feeling, the fans pulled off their own tops to sing it.

I felt the game wasn't quite as one sided as the score suggested – even at 3-0 up with 10 minutes to go, when Peterhead got the penalty, there was definitely a bit of nervousness about the Queens fans. In the end though it was the first time I'd ever seen Queens score five without reply in a competitive game. Fantastic.

Andy Paterson, Houston, Renfrewshire

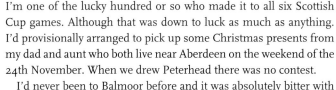

Queens vs. Peterhead away. Magic. Just the draw we wanted. We are struggling in the league and out of both the other cups. Not playing as well as I know we can and now we get Peterhead. Away. Magic.

The years of watching Queens have already prepared me for the potential disaster. I need to think about what excuses I will make at work if we go out. It's never easy up there. The ref was a homer. We just couldn't put the ball in the net. Years of practice. Easy.

I speak to a few of my mates. They feel the same. Couldn't have been worse. We will probably go out and not make any money from a cup run. Again. The rest of the season will be a relegation dog fight. Again. Football would bring nothing but disappointment. Again.

Then there was the realisation that none of us had seen Queens at Peterhead before. Let's go. Let's make a weekend of it. We'll stay in Aberdeen. A proper night out. Hotels, drink and discos. Magic. The cup starts here, we will put them to the sword then get an easy draw, who knows, could be the start of something special if we put in the effort and go. If we don't we will go out for sure and all we will see is the vidiprinter or hear James Alexander Gordon telling us that we are out.

Trains booked, bus links checked and the boys are going to Peterhead. The Big Man, Tin Man, Mucky, The Sieve, Walt and me. Six of us, three double rooms booked – I hope I am in with Mucky. Don't want to be sharing with The Big Man, he's a drinking machine.

We arrive at Queen Street at 7am. This is like a day at work not the weekend. Walt and The Sieve are getting a later train. The Big Man got us a deal on this so it's a tenner each. Magic.

Glasgow at that time on a Saturday morning is an odd place. It's like the city has a hangover. You can almost feel it. There are some odd people at the station. None odder than us I guess. One guy looks a right nutter, hope he doesn't sit with us.

We get on the train, The Big Man sits down, Mucky sits down, I sit down. The nutter is getting on our carriage. Quick Tin Man, sit down, don't give him the opportunity. Tin Man sits on his own, leaving the seat free. The nutter has sat down with us. I knew it. Magic.

The three of us look at Tin Man. He looks back as if to say it's all right. We all look at him to tell him it isn't. The nutter opens a can of lager. Its 7.30 am. Magic.

The nutter asks where we are off to. The nutter looks like if he doesn't get a reply he will smash our faces in. We tell him that we are off to see Queens play Peterhead and that we are worried that Queens will get beat. The nutter then asks Tin Man to buy him more lager as the guard has told him that he won't serve him any more. Tin Man agrees. Good call.

The nutter tells us that he is a Rangers fan and hates Aberdeen. He is only travelling up there to bring his brother back to Glasgow as his mad wife is ruining his brother's life. We nod in agreement. Good call boys. Thank God The Sieve isn't here; he'd probably tell the nutter that he has a cheek calling anyone else mad. The Sieve is like that.

The nutter tells us that Peterhead are absolute garbage. He tells us that we need to be more positive. He tells us that he supports Rangers and thinks that they can beat anyone. He tells us that Queens will beat Peterhead 5-0 and that there is nothing to worry about. He speaks with a conviction that is not to be disagreed with. Unless you want a fight with the nutter.

We tell him that Queens are not playing well. We tell him that we are out of both cups. We tell him that Queens have let us down over the years of going. We tell him that we would be happy just to go through. We tell him that it's not an easy place to go to. We tell him that we cannot see us winning 5-0.

He then asks us if we want a fight when we get off the train in Aberdeen. We decline. Thank God The Sieve isn't here. He would probably have got us in a fight on the train. The nutter laughs and says, 5-0, easy.

We get off the train and check into the hotel. The nutter is stopped by the guards at the station. We don't wait for him. By the time all this is done The Sieve and Walt have arrived, so we get on a bus to Peterhead. It's still a fair distance to go.

Balmoor. Another ground ticked off. Quite a nice little ground but a bit cold. In fact it's freezing. I thought it was bad at Montrose a few years ago but this is up there. Wish I was playing, running about would be better than watching today.

Bobby Mann. There he is. I can't stand him. I remember when he was at Forfar, and then at Inverness, I forgot he now played for Peterhead. He always plays well against Queens. Wish he wasn't playing. The nutter didn't know that, did he? 5-0 my arse, not with Mann playing.

It's a nice day. The game kicks off. Queens start quite well, looking confident. Peterhead look nervous. We need to score first, put them to the sword. That's what we need.

Mistake by Mann! It's as if the nutter has got into his head, Mann has been put off by something and made an awful error. Dobbs is in. Takes aim. Places it. Goal!!!! Queens are one up. Mann has his head in his hands due to that howler. Get it right up you Mann!

Tin Man is clapping above his head. Walt is banging the advertising boards. The Big Man is shouting to Mann to get it right up him. The Sieve is jumping up and down. Mucky is clenching a fist. We are on the way.

Two nil – O'Connor. Three nil – O'Connor. Four Nil – Dobbie. Five Nil – Burns. They even miss a penalty. No-one misses a penalty against Queens. The nutter is right. Queens have won five nil. We look at each other in amazement. Five nil. Maybe we have it all wrong and the nutter has it all right? We then cadge a lift back to Aberdeen on the Travel Club bus. The Sieve sorts it out and Ross lets us on.

We get to the hotel and get ready for a celebratory night out in Aberdeen. Queens have won five nil. We were all wrong and a nutter on the train drinking lager at 7.30 in the morning got the result and the score right. No wonder the bookies make so much money on football coupons.

We go to the boozer and wonder who we will get in the next round. We argue about getting one of the Old Firm away for money reasons or a home tie against non league opposition. We have a night out and think that you need to enjoy days like this.

We don't know that it will be the start of an incredible journey...

Fraser MacLean
Dumfries

CHAPTER 2
LINLITHGOW ROSE

Ran rings round the Rose

QUEEN OF THE SOUTH 4, LINLITHGOW ROSE 0

SATURDAY 12 JANUARY 2008
SCOTTISH CUP 4TH ROUND
Palmerston Park
QUEENS SCORERS: **Dobbie 16, Thomson 22, O'Connor 40,**
McArthur (og) 72
Attendance: **3,062**

QUEEN OF THE SOUTH

1	MacDonald
2	McCann
3	Harris
4	MacFarlane (**15** O'Neill, 80)
5	Aitken
6	Thomson
7	Gilmour
8	Tosh (**16** Paton, 82)
9	O'Connor
10	Dobbie (**14** Stewart, 75)
11	Burns
SUBS NOT USED:	
12	Grindlay
17	McQuilken

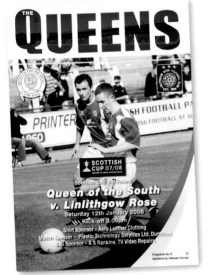

A good buzz about Palmerston for the historic Fourth Round meeting with Junior side Linlithgow Rose. Having suffered several embarrassing cup defeats to lower league opposition in my thirty years watching Queens it was pleasing to see how professionally and comfortably the match was won.

Gordon Harper

Dumfries

Fantastic atmosphere in the New Bazaar. We were in at 12.30 and the pub was heaving with much of the seating taken up by Linlithgow Rose fans. Many of the Rose fans had T-shirts saying "Kings of the East" and quite a few were wearing crowns. I know that 50 of them had booked in for breakfast at Weatherspoons for 9.00 a.m. but we felt it a privilege to be among this group. Mostly they were aged around 20-30 while most of the New Bazaar Doonhamers are 40-50 (mind you, the committee are somewhat older). I think I am right in saying that the many girls in the company were from some sort of sports club as most of the guys in the pub reckoned they were "fit" and some apparently were "well fit". Unfortunately I missed out on the group hugs where several of the young 'Roses' cuddled up to the older Queens fans for photo opportunities. Curse you all – I can't wait till I am also devoid of teeth and hair!!

Jim Harkness, Dumfries

It wasn't much past twelve noon and, as was usual on match days, myself and the other four usual suspects had already gathered at the public bar of the High Street Globe. Pints of lager and beer were going down spirits were both high and being knocked back when all of a sudden,

"scuse me mate, sorry auld pal, mind if I squeeze in there" filled the air. Linlithgow Rose had arrived in town. Ten minutes or so later the bar rush had all but died down and we, as true foot-ballin' kin folks do, had already become best friends.

The obligatory question and answer session started proceedings, "Why are you called Doonhamers", usual reply forthcoming."What's the story 'bout you lot, shoes and Bonnie Prince Charlie " again this was trotted out and over the next five minutes or so all the other usual questions followed on both sides, who was your best player, what was your best crowd etc. etc.

However as it is the way of these things the alcohol by now had started to kick in and of course someone felt a song coming on.

For our part the Railway Line started proceedings immediately followed by the Bonnie Banks. A half-hearted attempt to start off The Wheelbarrow song (Notts. County have a great deal to answer with this one) then began but thankfully they only managed two choruses and it faded away.

It was just after this moment when the Rose supporters began to sing their own songs, none of which I initially recognised, until curiously enough two of their fans started to repeat Ring a Ring o' Roses.

I asked one Rose supporter who was standing next to me how long they had been using this old song.

"dunno, been a long time though" came the reply, "think my dad will know though" he added

"haw dad, how long have we been singing this song, this man here wants tae know" I was right thumbed over his shoulder "dunno son, must be at least thirty maybe even forty years now, a long time anyway"

"there you go mate, must be at least forty years now, I kent it was a long time" he added

"right then thanks for that, but do you know the song is a lot older than that, in fact it was an old nursery rhyme and was being sung even as far back as the time of The Great Fire of London" I asked

" the whit"

"The Great Fire of London, 1666, sort of thing"

"nah it's no English mate its oors and it's no a weans song 'cause we're Juniors" he said, matter of fact.

I had no answer to this so I simply replied "Aye I suppose your right lad," and left it at that.

It has always been an interest of mine to note how words, phrases and songs come into general use and probably never more so than at that moment.

This song, this old nursery rhyme Ring a Ring o' Roses which started its life off as a lyrical description of Black Death, Bubonic Plague victims was now the adopted song of this small football club. No knowledge of the macabre history of this song was needed nor was it necessary because it was simply a song, their song and ultimately, in the grand scheme of things, I don't suppose there is too much wrong with that.

Scott Kerr, Dumfries

Linlithgow helped make the town maroon and white in a way only ever seen when Hearts come to town. They were a friendly bunch and many followed our results from there on in. Full credit to them.

Stuart Rae, Dumfries

CHAPTER 3
MORTON

Made light work of the 'Ton

MORTON 0, QUEEN OF THE SOUTH 2

SATURDAY 2 FEBRUARY 2008
SCOTTISH CUP 5TH ROUND
Cappielow Park
QUEENS SCORERS: **O'Connor 46, Stewart 87**
Attendance: **3,506**

QUEEN OF THE SOUTH

1	MacDonald
2	McCann
3	Harris
4	MacFarlane
5	Aitken
6	Thomson
7	McQuilken
8	Tosh
9	O'Connor (**15** O'Neill, 68)
10	Dobbie (**14** Stewart, 75)
11	Burns

SUBS NOT USED:

12	Grindlay
16	Paton
17	Gilmour

One memory of Queens cup run was the 5th round on the 2nd February on a dreary wet day at Cappielow when Queens beat Morton 2-0. There were several hundred Queens fans with many of the young team standing in the downpour because there was no room left in the visitors' stand. They all sang their hearts out and we had the added bonus of a stripper on the terracing in the pouring rain.

Eric Fisher
Dumfries

An anxious start to the day logged on to the internet awaiting confirmation that the Cappielow pitch was playable. Second hurdle to overcome was the "only travel if absolutely necessary" weather forecast. However a Queens away game (and especially a Scottish Cup tie) usually falls into the essential journey category. Packed my wellies and a shovel in the boot of the car to counter any weather difficulties and then picked up my passengers and it was off to Greenock.

The snow made for a scenic run up the M74 with only a small section of road proving to be treacherous. Stopped off at Tesco in Port Glasgow for lunch and was pleased to see the café fill up with Queens fans and a member of the Board of Directors! Plenty of good Queens chat ensued and we left for our destination quietly confident of a successful outcome to the match.

Gordon Harper
Dumfries

February the second, 2008 was the day Queen of the South's love affair with the Scottish Cup began. It was also the day my love-hate affair began with Jim Traynor, from Radio Scotland. If being honest when I opened my curtains that morning I couldn't have seen the trip to Greenock further – it was peeing down but deep down inside I had a strange feeling this was going to be a cup classic – plus I could pop into Ikea on the way.

So after a two-hour drive through the rain and wind, we arrived at Cappielow and were directed into the car park, but as I stepped outside the car and landed ankle deep in a puddle I began to think maybe this wasn't going to be quite the day I was hoping for. We then walked around the far side of the stadium to be greeted with a huge queue and only two turnstiles open. Unfortunately one of them was a family gate. After a good 20 minute wait the Doonhamers were getting restless and thoughts of the League Cup game against Hibernian in 2003, where the organisers underestimated our support by a mere 1500, were on our mind. However as the kick-off approached the ingenuity of the good people of Dumfries shone through the dank miserable day as punters borrowed children from each other so they could get through the family gate. Not having that option and fearing we were never going to get in, I chanced my arm, popped the exact money down and was let through – and boy was I glad – the heavens opened further, and we were about the last people to get a seat in the covered stand.

As the game started Queens' fans continued to pour through the turnstiles and with no room left in the stand they huddled together on the terracing behind the goal. Undeterred by the weather they sang their wee hearts out – many choosing to give two-fingers to the rain by doing so with their tops off, for reasons I'll never understand. One guy even went so far as to remove his jeans too and was later promptly lifted by the local police after his mate yanked down his boxers to reveal all (not that there was much to see).

Fortunately, unlike the fans on the terracing, both teams were totally focussed on the game – and what a game it was. Despite having supported old favourite Peter 'Elephant Man' Weatherson in the previous round as Morton demolished Gretna – all former allegiances were off. Weatherson had already had a taste of what he's been missing since leaving Palmerston, when we beat Morton 3-0 in the league a few weeks earlier – but cup games bring out special performances and we knew not to underestimate them.

Both teams were fired up for what turned out to be a classic cup game with each putting in a gritty and determined performance, and the fans were treated to end-to-end action. Despite a nervy moment in the first half when an excellent Weatherson header was tipped over the bar by an equally excellent Jamie MacDonald save, the first half finished goalless. The rain continued to teem down in the second half but it didn't dampen the fire in either set of players and within a minute Queens were a goal up courtesy of Sean O'Connor.

Morton continued to exert pressure on us and despite the lead the game still felt like anybody's, and the nerves of both sets of fans were clear to see. Finally, in the closing minutes the game was put to bed with a late John Stewart goal and 700 Doonhamers set off on the journey home with smiles on their faces and a sense of expectation in our hearts. Two years, two quarter-finals – could we dream of getting to the semis and to Hampden?

With a long journey home ahead of us we tuned into Your Call with Jim Traynor, and despite the fact that it was a cup weekend and that neither of the Old Firm had actually played we were subjected to the inane dribblings of a selection of cerebrally challenged Old Firm fans, moaning as usual.

Motivated by this I sent in a text reminding the alleged 'Airdrie Fan' of these facts, finishing my text with 'Bring on Hampden'. The text was duly read out on air to be met with snorts of derision from Jim who claimed that even if we did get through we would be lucky to take 100 fans to Hampden (despite the fact we had just taken 700 to Morton). How dare he! Who did he think we were.... Gretna?

But his petty and ill-informed opinions didn't faze us, and from that moment on I knew this was going to be the special season it turned out to be – and to quote Jim Traynor himself from his cup final report in the Daily Record ....

'GORDON Chisholm, his Queen of the South players and their fans were Hampden stars on Saturday. They didn't win anything other than respect but they made cup final day special, even if they didn't quite seize it. The Dumfries side were followed to the National Stadium by 16,000 supporters and every one of them seemed determined to enjoy the occasion.'

That is what football is all about Jim. And yes, you are sometimes wrong.

Get it right up ye!

Joanna Wright
Dumfries

We had just passed Abington when the road became single lane on each carriageway. The window wipers on the New Bazaar Doonhamers mininbus struggled to clear the snow as the blizzard worsened. I was surprised that no-one suggested we abort the trip. When we left Dumfries we knew there would be a pitch inspection but we did not know when. Why did we bother? We knew the weather forecast was grim. We could not get signals on our mobile phones and wondered what to do. "Turn back" came the cry from... er nobody. Even though the M74 was only passable on one lane in each direction we pressed on. When we got to Larkhall the snow was sparse and we began to feel as if our day was not going to be wasted. By the time we arrived at our favoured howff (the 'Fox and Hounds' at Houston) our spirits were high. Then, after a few pints of '1919 Doonhamers Ale' we were in the right frame of mind to force a win! We did – 2-0

Jim Harkness
Dumfries

The week before the 5th round game, we still didn't know if it was Gretna or Morton we would be playing away. Due to the farcical ground conditions at Fir Park where Gretna were playing their home games, the Gretna v Morton game was to be played at Palmerston. I'd a hunch that Morton would beat Gretna and as we had just beaten Morton 3-0 at Cappielow, felt we had a good chance of progressing. As a fair number of SPL teams had gone out already, there was a 50:50 or so chance of drawing a lower league team if we progressed. Queens at that point were 400-1 to win the cup, so I sneaked a fiver each way on – you never know!!

As it happened, the Morton game was probably the least memorable of the cup run, coming two weeks after we beat them in the league with Dobbie getting a hat-trick in that game after coming on as a sub. He couldn't match the feat in the cup game but we won comfortably enough 2-0, and I got a ride home in a car with a Morton fan so the banter was flying.

Andy Paterson
Houston, Renfrewshire

With a forecast of inclement weather in the Greenock area it was time to hunt out the long black coat that had hung in the back of my wardrobe before boarding a Travel Club bus to Cappielow and the Scottish Cup tie against Morton.

An uneventful journey saw us arrive at the Greenock teams' social club which is a fair distance from the ground and in we piled to what reminded me of an old-fashioned village hall with tables and chairs around the walls. The place was heaving and the small bar in the corner was run off its feet by the thirsty Doonhamer support. After a few pints and a couple of free, traditional, 'dripping in grease' pies we were off to the game and it was soon apparent that Queens had a big support on the day as a long queue formed at the turnstiles with rain pouring down. Once ensconced in the stand it was funny to see the "young team' from Dumfries standing on the uncovered terracing getting drooked – some without shirts and one who was momentarily naked before the local Old Bill removed him from the ground.

Half-time came and the old bladder was full to capacity but the toilets at Cappielow are a long way from the stand. However this is where my long, black coat came into play. A steward was turning all the Queens fans away and pointing them to the distant toilet but as I went forward (with no colours on) he obviously thought I was a businessman-type and waved me through to a lounge where corporate diners were enjoying a half-time swally. No-one gave me a second glance and I casually strolled through to the obviously better class of toilet thanks to my L.B.C.

Bruce L. Wright
Dumfries

Morton was a great away day out. It gave all at the New Bazaar Doonhamers the opportunity to make our third pre-match visit of the season to the Fox & Hounds pub in Houston (not far from Greenock) and we were back again on cup final day where a warm welcome is always extended from the owner who is a big St Mirren fan.

The pub has its very own in-house brewery with a selection of ales, and produced the 1919 Doonhamers Ale sold in the New Bazaar during our cup run. Two weeks earlier at the same ground we were all going 'mental' when Stephen Dobbie scored a great hat-trick within less than 20 minutes of coming on as a sub (days after signing a new contract). This prompted the one and only 'Brian Kelly' to come up with a new song about "away away, we'll be there when Stephen Dobbie scores away away" 10,000 chants later we can't get rid of it from our brains. No such luck for Dobbie this time but we did win 2-0 with John Stewart finally managing to get on the score sheet (and a bigger goal was to follow from him). Laughs aloud for the stripper on the terracing behind the goals.

Stuart Rae
Dumfries

CHAPTER 4
DUNDEE

Then double 'Dees (a great pair)

QUEEN OF THE SOUTH 2, DUNDEE 0

SATURDAY 8 MARCH 2008
SCOTTISH CUP QUARTER-FINAL
Palmerston Park
QUEENS SCORERS: **Dobbie 51, McCann 90**
Attendance: **6,278**

QUEEN OF THE SOUTH

1	MacDonald
2	McCann
3	Harris
4	MacFarlane
5	Aitken
6	Thomson
7	McQuilken
8	Tosh
9	O'Connor
10	Dobbie (**14** Stewart, 78)
11	Burns

SUBS NOT USED:

12	Grindlay
15	O'Neill
16	Gilmour
17	Paton

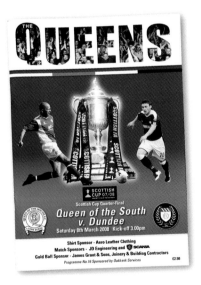

"May I thank the Chairman, his fellow board members, the manager and his staff, and all the squad for the journey they have taken us all on so far, and wish them all the very best for Saturday. Do your best – we can expect no more than that. Do so, and if we carry that little bit of luck, you can take us to where few of us ever dreamed of, and you will be remembered by Queens fans forever. Best of luck to you all."

Mark McMinn, Dumfries

Quarter-final day and Palmerston was heaving, although the Queens fans were strangely subdued for much of the game. Perhaps the weight of expectation and anticipation had enveloped the ground. Cue Stephen Dobbie early in the second half and then Ryan McCann's marvellous 84-yard wonder strike. One of the best moments in my 30-odd years supporting Queens and also for my mate Mark McCreadie, who later had "McCann 84" printed on the back of his Queens top.

I remember screaming in my car as I waited for the sea of vehicles to file out of the car park, "We're going to Hampden", listening to the radio interviews just to confirm it was true.

And then, moments later, the draw is made and we face either Aberdeen or Celtic.

The long car journey home to Elgin 24 hours later ends with radio commentary of the Dons-Celtic clash and a late-late equaliser for the Glasgow giants. I had been relishing a match-up with Aberdeen, surrounded as I am at work and in the wider community by Dons fans.

I couldn't believe it when Aberdeen came up with a stunning replay win.

The following morning I nip into work a bit early and adorn one of my Aberdeen-supporting colleagues' desk with Queens memorabilia. The war of words has started in earnest.

Chris Saunderson

Elgin

I'm one of the many exiled Doonhamers; in my case, I live in Bebington on the Wirral (not far from Liverpool). Despite being around three hours from Dumfries, I try to get to as many games as possible. My wife (who's French) is now an avid Queens fan and we've managed to get to 23 games in this past season. Many of my work colleagues and students (I'm a secondary school teacher) think I'm crazy, but I think they've now started to realise that perhaps after this season, it's all been worth it.

I don't think I've ever experienced such a rush of emotions as I did during the amazing cup run. Ryan McCann's wonderstrike resulted in me dancing in the aisles of the main stand at Palmerston with a man I'd only met some 90 minutes earlier. The realisation that we were on our way to Hampden was way too much for me as I completely broke down and cried tears of joy when the final whistle went. In the future, I'll always be able to claim, "I was there when Ryan McCann scored from 84 yards to take Queens through to only their second ever Scottish Cup semi-final." Davie Rae's exuberance at the final whistle was a joy to behold; that man typifies everything I love about my 'hame team'.

Chris McKie
Bebington, Wirral

The pub was jumping. The Dundee fans inside were in fine form and good voice. They insisted on singing a vast repertoire of songs extolling the virtues of Charlie Cooke, Alan Gilzean and the like. However the New Bazaar Doonhamers were tooled up (with fully waxed rattles!) and copies of the Sun (that day, the 'Sun' had done a feature on 'the Rattlers' and had in fact made them front page (in colour) on their Saturday supplement). After a few choruses from the Dundee fans the NBD (led by Brian) erupted with "You're not famous any more!!" while waving copies of the Saturday supplement! The Dundee fans tried to respond with the same old dirges but they were drowned out by 20 or so rattles raising the roof! One Dundee fan (later filmed topless by the BBC) complained that we could have been carded due to ungentlemanly conduct. He had a point!!

Jim Harkness
Dumfries

There are many reasons why I don't like Dundee Football Club: their arrogant belief they should be in the SPL; the skewed 1st Division media coverage in their favour; Alex Rae (self explanatory); and the fact that they have just poached one of my favourite players Eric Paton. Oh aye, and I have to admit I've had a soft spot for the Arabs since I was a child, which may have coloured my opinion slightly.

That aside, they always give us a good game. On Boxing Day ex-Doonhamer Derek Lyle was red-carded and with a 2-1 victory Queens got back to winning ways. We followed this with a 3-2 win over them in January and, with Rae and Chisholm sharing the Manager of the Month Award for February, the cup game was shaping up to be a good one. I have to admit I was nervous – in fact, on reflection, more so than when we had to face Aberdeen and Rangers in later rounds.

The match was scrappy, and a nervy watch for both sets of fans. I believe Dundee had a few good chances to score but all I remember are the two Queens' goals. Dobbie made goal scoring look effortless and I'll never forget my sense of relief and joy as he slotted home and then rounded the pitch with his arms held out like a child playing aeroplanes (an image that has adorned my laptop ever since). And who could have known the best was yet to come. There isn't anything new left to say about Ryan McCann's 84-yard clincher. From my seat in the main stand it seemed to take forever to travel the length of the pitch and as it trundled over the line, there was one added bonus from my seat – Alex Rae's face.

Class.

Joanna Wright
Dumfries

Before Dundee were relegated in 2005 I'd struggle to tell you anything about Queen of the South but over the last three seasons I've learned a thing or two.

Of our eight long trips (longer on the way home) we've won once. That win came in a meaningless end of season game, we've lost four and drawn three. One of those draws resulted in extra time and then not surprisingly us being beaten on penalties.

You'd think from these memories that Dundee would travel to Palmerston expecting to get beat but something about the cup took over and we set off full of confidence with a trip to Hampden in our sights.

As we arrived in Dumfries and got chatting to some Queens fans it was clear to see how much this meant to their support and their club.

There is something you can't help but like about the club even though we cannot seem to find a way to beat them.

As the match started that confidence had turned into nerves that only a cup game can create and by half time I was happy to settle for a 0-0 draw and take Queens to a replay at Dens.

One man had other ideas though and one of those things I have learned about Queen of the South since we got relegated is they have a man called Stephen Dobbie who you don't really want to be giving any space around your box. Seven minutes into the second half and he was given that space and with two perfect touches we were 1-0 down and now looking a long way from that replay I was settling for at half time.

We pushed on but didn't seem to be getting anywhere and were gifted a golden opportunity to get the ball into the box in the form of a free kick out wide. Our keeper Craig Samson made his way into the area and as the ball ricocheted around the last place we wanted it to fall was at a Queens players feet. Looking back now more specifically Ryan McCann's feet.

Queens fans won't need any explanation of the goal but as the ball sailed the 80 yards or so into the net and I slumped back into my chair, I sampled the bad times of the cup as I watched the home fans on the terracing celebrate the good.

You'd think after this the last thing I'd want to do is cheer Queens on in their semi-final but as I said earlier there is something you can't help but like about them. I took great joy watching them overcome Aberdeen then give Rangers the shock of a lifetime.

I bet you they have both learned a thing or two about Queen of the South now too.

Tommy Young, Dundee Supporter

Never had we had such a great chance to make the semi-final and on the back of our great unbeaten run we all "believed". We were in heaven when Dobbie scored but despite controlling the game nails were bitten aplenty in the final minutes until that goal... Ryan McCann's 84 yard strike must surely have been greeted by some of the greatest scenes ever seen at Palmerston. With the Dundee goalie up the park I remember shouting jokingly to 'shoot' as the ball fell to McCann. As always we were on the terracing behind the goal and as the ball came towards us the whole crowd seemed to be almost sucking the ball in. I feared it would stick in the muddy patch in the six yard box but as everyone went wild we realised it was going in. To say the scenes were 'wild and jubilant' was the understatement of the century. I was literally seeing 'stars' as I went absolutely stark raving bonkers and had hardly stopped jumping up and down when the final whistle went.

For about half an hour afterwards I thought I was going to pass out. I reckon the adrenalin rush on that goal would have killed an elephant stone dead. I have had many wild celebrations in my 33 years of following Queens but up to that point that was the best. Great celebrations thereafter. On the Monday back at work I turned up for my 12-8pm shift to find others were having a bad day. When asked why I was so 'happy' I explained that I'd had one of the greatest experiences of my life on Saturday.

"Why did you jump out of an aeroplane, or something?" came one reply. There were looks of stunned and almost apologetic silence when I explained that it was celebrating Queens second goal (you know the 'you must get out more' look). I didn't care as the people I work directly with are not Queens fans and generally not football fans so like my wife and many others they will never get close to understanding what it meant to me. One colleague did try and claim a level of understanding by saying she knew what it meant to Rangers or Celtic fans when they were watching a match between each other in the pub (nice try but that would never be a close comparison in a million years).

Stuart Rae, Dumfries

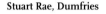

A strong sense of "this is the day" amongst supporters in the main stand prior to kick off. This was due to our winning run and our good record against Dundee in the league. Would we finally triumph in a big match in front of a packed crowd at Palmerston? Too right we did – another class finish from Stephen Dobbie and what can I add to what will already have been written about Ryan McCann's 84-yard goal other than as the crowd celebrated as the ball bounced towards the net some fans thought the referee had blown for full time. Just having calmed down from that goal the final whistle did sound and we all went crazy again!

Gordon Harper
Dumfries

A tense first half: not a pretty game of football plus I was close enough to the front to be caught in the downpour of rain/sleet/hail, so not only was I nervous, but soaked as well. However, the second half made up for the bout of pneumonia that followed. In it I saw two of the most fantastic goals I will ever remember.

The first, route 1 from Jamie MacD. to Dobbie. He took a touch then pelted it with the right side of his foot and it was in! Big celebrations. Owen and I lost Bill (father-in-law) in the bedlam. We watched the game and the time tick away. Owen and I banned each other from looking at our watches.

Tension rose as Dundee got a free kick. We commented that Samson (keeper) had gone up front. We wait.

The kick is taken, but we can't see what happens. Frantically trying to work out where the ball is, we finally see it as McCann clears it.

It takes a few seconds for it to sink in:

it's not a clearance – it's a shot! Time stands still. The ball approaches. It hits the ground once. There is a patch of mud... Twice... We all breathe in... Third bounce and in!! Wild celebrations. Did we all "sook" the ball over the line?

Robbie Purdie
Dumfries

I booked a holiday to Cancun in late Feb/March, and it was only at the last minute I realised that I would miss the quarter-final v Dundee. The thought of trading night-clubs like Coco Bongos and the delights of American college girls on spring break, for Palmerston did cross my mind but I decided to head off to Mexico anyway. The Saturday of the game I was wandering round the beach with a bunch of Barnsley fans at 10.30am Mexican time trying to find bars with Espn/Skysports/Setanta – I was hoping for BBC Scotland but thought that would be a longshot. Began to sober up and realise that Central America may not share my enthusiasm for QOS and the chance of a live broadcast was slim.

Eventually a Mexican bar owner offered me his laptop to check the scores – 1-0 to Queens – I danced around the bar cheering like mad (Corona is a wonderful thing), singing "Queens are going to Hampden". It was only then one of my group pointed out there was still 20 minutes to go (I'd got my times all wrong). An anxious 20 minutes followed with me checking Skysports.com religiously, then in injury time the news I wanted was there 2-0 Queens scorer Neil MacFarlane, I was shocked that Neil had scored but delighted, the scoreline was then corrected – arggghh! surely not a Dundee equaliser, but then saw it was just corrected to McCann.

Suddenly Mexico seemed dull compared

to Dumfries. An all day session came after and last thing I can remember is myself, three Barnsley fans, a Brummie and a Hearts fan chanting "we hate Gretna" across the lagoon in Senor Frogs Bar. Even the locals were joining in though they didn't have a clue what I was singing about.

The next day I was flying home and spent 10 hours stranded at Gatwick due to high winds, I spent £14 quid in the internet cafe watching McCann's goal over and over again! Queens are going to Hampden!!! That goal will always remind me of two of the best times of my life, a wonderful holiday and Queens amazing cup run.

Scot Carrick
Dumfries

As I'm based in the Central Belt, the trip to Palmerston for the Dundee quarter-final was a longer one than to Cappielow. Dundee brought a decent crowd and the game was more or less a sell-out. Sadly the banter from some of the Dundee fans was a bit less savoury than the Linlithgow supporters as the Tayside hordes took over the pubs near the ground. The game will be remembered for the Ryan McCann 84 yarder which sends a shiver down the spine whenever I look at a replay. The match was so tense that Ryan's goal coming as it did in the last minute sent us all into mental mode. The first Scottish Cup semi-final for 58 years (I'm only 40 so the first ever for me)!

Andy Paterson, Houston, Renfrewshire

Myself and my mate Stuart Fair (who is as blind as a bat and has to wear glasses at all times) were stood behind the goal at the Dundee game when Ryan McCann shot home from 84 yards.

As soon as the ball left his boot I had a funny feeling it was going in and started to jump all over Stuart in celebration.

After the ball reached the net and the ensuing mayhem settled down I looked at Stuart and he was nowhere to be seen. Stuart, a lifelong Queens fan, was crawling about the ground trying to find his glasses. He resurfaced in tears (a mix of tears of joy and tears of sadness). Stuart a man who I have known for many years and have never known to swear turned to me and said " Ya big b*****d I have followed Queens all my life and missed the goal that takes them to the semi-finals at Hampden as you knocked my glasses off when you started celebrating before the ball went in ".

Iain Dalling, Dumfries

It all started to get silly when the Tan Man plunged through a coffee table. Dundee were already going to be missing the better half of their team due to injury and suspension by the time they'd disposed of the best Motherwell side in a generation for us. But when the striker who was bound to score against us again, took himself out of the reckoning in such comic fashion, (denying all rumours that he'd been attempting to make love to his reflection) it was all clearly going too well. People were getting so optimistic about our prospects against Dundee in the quarter-final that it engendered a deep sense of pessimism. My wife and dad wanted to attend this one, so in what became a habit, I arranged to buy tickets. The fact that my dad's a Dundee fan, reared on Gilzean, Ure and Co complicated matters a bit and he chose to stand quietly with a pal twenty yards from the rest of us. Windy would probably describe the game itself as adequately as any other adjective. The first half blew away quickly, before MacDonald started the second with a save every bit as good as the fumble which preceded it had been bad. The stress levels only really soared after we took the lead though. Dobbie did what he does controlling a ball dropping from on high to knock it classily into the corner. From here on in, it was no fun whatsoever. Dundee didn't offer a great deal, but we sat deep and let them try. The problem with this match was that for us, the stakes were so high. We'd reached the quarter-finals the year before – our first in thirty odd years but were always likely then to lose to Hibs. This time though, we were playing a team from our league which we'd beaten recently and they were depleted. We knew we had a great chance of reaching a semi-final, of playing at Hampden, of being live on TV. Therefore we had to screw up. When John Stewart broke clear for us and missed a one-on-one, I just knew that Dundee would punish us and that Stewart would ever more be remembered by Queens fans for costing us a semi-final place.

I've now watched the free kick Dundee got at the end so often on TV, that I'm not entirely sure what I recall from the moment itself and what I've filled in since. I do remember the Dundee attack coming to nothing and the ball then being punted clear when I was screaming for it to be held. And then the ball was flying towards us. And we were behind the unguarded goal so that meant... At first my wife wasn't sure what it meant she didn't know if you were allowed to score from there. As it went in, everyone indulged in the type of frenzied, fluid celebrating that makes you glad Palmerston's not SPL compliant. You just can't go daft like that in seats. The Dundee fans who didn't linger to throw things on the pitch duly filed to the exits, granting us the opportunity of a lusty version of o'Cheerio, Cheerio, Cheerio!" and then it finished. Even Dad was pleased for us.

Geoff Leonard, Dumfries

A couple of weeks after the quarter-final Tie v Dundee, the New Bazaar Doonhamers 'exam' took place. In the Queens team that night was goal hero Ryan McCann and the following question seemed perfect for them... "Think back to Ryan McCann's 84 yard wonder goal against Dundee. How many times did the ball bounce before it crossed the line?" The Queens team got this one wrong and blamed their error on Ryan McCann. They were of course pilloried for this with one wit exclaiming.."Why did you listen to him? – He was furthest away!!!"

Jim Harkness
Dumfries

CHAPTER 5
ABERDEEN

Jimmy C's flock were Tango'd

QUEEN OF THE SOUTH 4, ABERDEEN 3

SATURDAY 12 APRIL 2008
SCOTTISH CUP SEMI-FINAL
Hampden Park
QUEENS SCORERS: **Tosh 22, Burns 49, O'Connor 56, Stewart 60**
Attendance: **24,008**

QUEEN OF THE SOUTH

1 MacDonald
2 McCann (**16** Paton, 90)
3 Harris
4 MacFarlane
5 Aitken
6 Thomson
7 McQuilken
8 Tosh
9 O'Connor
10 Dobbie (**14** Stewart, 42)
11 Burns

SUBS NOT USED:

12 Grindlay
15 O'Neill
17 Gilmour

It's 58 years since we were in a Scottish Cup semi-final and now we are in a final. We would get our noses in front and give another goal away and it just went on and on. I thought Aberdeen would come back for the fourth time and the game could have been 6-5 or 7-4.

Gordon Chisholm
Manager
Queen of the South FC

As a result of exortations on the Doonhamers Mad website, many Queens fans wore kilts to the semi-final. As we queued at the turnstiles one of the New Bazaar Doonhamers spoke to an XXL guy in front and complimented him on his kilt. "Is that yer ain?" he asked "Aye". "What's the tartan?" the NBD guy asked. "McDonald" the bloke with the waistline responded and then he added "but I have to say my family link with the McDonald's is prettty tenuous". "Right" said the NBD guy "So you just eat a lot of burgers then?"

Jim Harknesss
Dumfries

The week leading up to the big game had me on the same emotional rollercoaster of nerves and excitement as the Scotland vs Italy Euro 2008 decider back in November. Fortunately the outcome was better this time – better than I could have ever imagined. Time stood still for the last twenty minutes or so, but 10,000 of us were there witnessing the greatest victory in the history of the club.

Gordon Harper
Dumfries

No sleep on Friday night, like a kid on Christmas Eve, dreaming a variety of scorelines and scenarios the following morning but never 4-3 for Queens. I travelled to Hampden with the Travel Club and the scene at Palmerston beforehand was amazing.

The weather was pretty amazing too and resembled more of a winter's day on the journey to Glasgow. We arrived there early and soaked up the atmosphere, happily mingling with Dons fans, except for one who was slightly boozed up and decided to pinch my large floppy hat, although it was returned moments later.

A phone call from my Aberdeen-supporting colleague sent me in the direction of The International Bar. "It's full of reds", he says, "but you'll be safe enough". I felt like a lamb to the slaughter as I passed legions of Aberdeen fans – a solitary blue-clad supporter against a tide of red. Regular chants of "Who ate all the pies" (the years have not been good to my waistline) were taken on the chin before I reached the bar.

A few beers, paid for by my Dons mate, and I beat a hasty retreat back to Hampden for a game that will live long in the memory.

A rollercoaster second half simply rained goals and at one point I thought I was going to pass out my blood pressure was so high.

A quick text at the end: "Well done mate, you deserved it" from my Aberdeen pal summed up the sporting nature of the occasion.

Chris Saunderson, Elgin

Saturday 12 April 2008 – a day and an occasion that many Queens fans never believed they would see – Queen of the South against Aberdeen in the semi-final of the Scottish Cup. This would be Queens playing in front of an estimated 11,000 fans in the 26,000 crowd at Hampden and the match being broadcast around the world on Sky TV in what was also Queens first ever live game on TV. The last time Queens had reached the semi-final was in 1950, 58 years ago and had never reached the final in their 89-year history.

In recent years Queens had played several SPL teams in the Scottish Cup, only last season they were unlucky to go down to a good Hibernian team 2-1 and in 2003 drew 0-0 against Aberdeen at Palmerston Park only to lose the replay 4-1 in Aberdeen. Although playing well in these two matches there had been a number of howlers as well, losing 3-0 to Dundee United at Palmerston, Motherwell 3-2 at Fir Park after allowing Motherwell a 3-0 half time lead and a mid-week CIS League Cup game against Hibs when two early goals finished the tie within the first 20 minutes. On the latter three occasions despite playing in front of a big Queens support the general opinion was the team had not performed. What Queen's team would turn out today?

Aberdeen had been a bit hit or miss all season. On their day they could beat anyone and equally lose to anyone. Which Aberdeen team would turn up today? Hopefully the latter. Queens were given a boast with news that Sean O'Connor had been passed fit to start the match after being carried off in a league match against Morton two weeks before. Despite a journey north from Dumfries-shire through snow and sleet it was very noticeable that the Queens support were in and around the ground long before the start. This was our 'cup final'. We wanted to soak up the atmosphere. If only the team could do ourselves justice.

The noise as the teams came out was deafening and just a mass of blue and white at our end and red and white at the Aberdeen end. Aberdeen would be playing towards the Queens support during the first half. If only we can keep it tight at the back for the first 15-20 mins to gave us time to settle and play ourselves into the match. Then perhaps we could sneak a goal and win one nil or take the

game to penalties. How would Dobbie and O'Connor last the pace and how would the ageing midfield of Tosh and MacFarlane deal with the big Hampden pitch?

It took 22 minutes before Queens took the lead. A long free kick from McCann was not held by Aberdeen keeper Soutar before the ball broke to Tosh to hammer home into the top corner. The Queens support who had been singing and encouraging their team magnificently were on their feet in a mass of blue and white. Queens had taken the lead; even if we get beat now we had scored at Hampden and had actually taken the lead against an SPL team. Can we hold out for 68 minutes?

Keep it tight for the next 10 minutes and don't concede a soft goal. Bad news was to follow when Dobbie went to the sidelines to get treatment for a leg knock. With O'Connor just getting back from a two-week lay off it was vital our top goalscorer remained on the field to lead the strike partnership.

Aberdeen were putting Queens under extreme pressure and with the help of 11,000 supporters heading and clearing every opportunity it was disappointing when Aberdeen did eventually equalise through Considine in

36 minutes when he rose above Jim Thomson. Worse was to follow when Dobbie signalled to the bench he could not continue and was replaced by John Stewart (who had previously been discarded by Aberdeen). One of our potential penalty takers now off the field. If only we can get to half time without conceding another that would be an achievement.

After 45 minutes the referee did blow the whistle to give the Queens supporters a chance to relax but they continued to sing all through the half-time break. Met a pal during the interval who had followed Queens threw thick and thin for many years, what did he think of Queens first goal at Hampden? – He missed it as he had had a few too many beers on the way to the match and had to content himself with watching it on the TV screens above the pie stalls. I think everyone was pleased with the way the game had gone, good to have scored, shame about equaliser but still belief we could pinch a goal or win on penalties. The important thing was to keep it tight for the first 15 minutes of the second half.

In 49 minutes what was arguably the best goal I have seen at Hampden. Harris picked up the ball in ➡

his own half and played it up along the line, O'Connor did a dummy that allowed Stewart to go belting past and down the wing with the right back trailing behind him. What was even better was that Paul Burns was sprinting through the middle almost unmarked. A cross from Stewart would be met by Burns surely. After what seemed like a lifetime Stewart did cross the ball towards Burns. Burns had a simple strike at the ball to make it two-one but somehow he miscontrolled the ball (hands in head time at missed opportunity) before the ball broke to him again and this time he made no mistake as he curled the ball past Soutar in the Aberdeen goal. Again the support were on their feet applauding and supporting another goal. Queens had scored twice at Hampden to be leading 2-1, now to keep it tight and take the sting out of the game. Can we hold out for 41 minutes?

Aberdeen had not read the game plan and struck back four minutes later. A badly defended cross allowed Doonhamer Barry Nicholson to blast home from close range. After taking the game to Aberdeen and taking the lead Queens had lost a cheap goal within four minutes of scoring. The fans went quiet for a spell before a rousing noise got up trying to encourage the team forward. After all Queens had scored twice against Aberdeen.

Two minutes later a long ball from MacDonald in the Queens goal was misjudged by an Aberdeen defender at edge of the centre circle. As quick as a flash O'Connor was on to it and running towards goal. As two defenders started to close O'Connor down as he reached the edge of the box he got his shot away and beat Soutar for a third goal. O'Connor made straight for the Queens support near the corner flag who were out of their seats again singing and chanting. Incredible that Queens had scored a third goal and were now leading 3-2 within 11 minutes of half time. The stuff of dreams. Now if only we could keep it tight at the back for 10-15 minutes and not allow Aberdeen back into the game as we had after the second.

Strange as it seems in Aberdeen's next attack they scored when Miller headed across goal for Considine to score his second and bring the score back level. Queens support were gutted in disbelief, three times Queens had taken a lead only for Aberdeen to pull back and twice in the second half they could not hold onto the lead for more than two minutes. If you had told any Queen's supporter before the match they would score three against Aberdeen within an hour they would have gladly taken it.

This time it was Queens turn to score within a minute. A McCann throw in was played back to him; his cross allowed Thomson to flick the ball on at the near post to an unmarked John Stewart who just belted the ball as hard as he could towards the Aberdeen goal. As the ball left Stewart's foot the Queens support were on their feet and micro seconds later the ball hit the back of the net. It was hit so hard Soutar did not see it although if he had got a touch to it I am sure it would have been deflected past the goal, so hard was it hit. Again Stewart (who hadn't had the best goalscoring record for Queens) headed straight for the Queens fans as the rest of the players congratulated him. Queens supporters could not believe this, it was fantasy football at its best. If only we could keep it tight at the back and not allow Aberdeen another goal. To score four goals against an SPL side was beyond our wildest dreams but the defence needed to be stronger.

Five goals in 15 minutes, if this scoring rate kept up it would 10-9 by full-time. At this time I was texting the scorers to my brother after each goal – I think he thought I was on a wind up. To think Queens had not scored in their last three league matches and now four against Aberdeen. One minute you were on such a high with a place in the final ours only for it to be snatched away within a few minutes. We didn't even have time to enjoy the goals and leading before Aberdeen levelled. The other main issue was that Jimmy Calderwood took off a full back to replace with a forward as they went all out for another equaliser.

The moment I really thought we may win this match came at the 73 minute mark when Zander Diamond headed against the Queens crossbar only for the rebound to fall to his feet when he hit it off MacDonald's left hand post. It's at moments like these you think this could be it. Another telling moment came in the last 10 minutes when big Jim Thomson made a perfect tackle on the Aberdeen striker in the box when from a distance you thought a penalty could be given despite 14,000 Aberdeen fans telling the referee a different version.

The fourth official held up a board indicating 4 minutes of injury time, where did he find the extra time? This was not good news for Queens, as in recent weeks they had conceded late goals to Livingston, St Johnstone and Hamilton and who could forget the opening match of the season when they let a 3-1 lead slip in injury time against St Johnstone. Thankfully most of the action took place right in front of us as Tosh and O'Connor took the ball walkabouts into the corner. Aberdeen had one last chance as Nicholson found acres of space within the penalty box but hit his shot straight at MacDonald. At this stage Chisholm made another change taking off 84-yard semi-final hero Ryan McCann but the only reason being he was the furthest away player from the dugout at the time.

The referee blew for full-time, which started the most amazing celebration on the Hampden pitch. Every Queens player congratulated each other as backroom staff and Davie Rae applauded the fans. Indeed a large number of Aberdeen supporters stayed behind to applaud the Queens team. No one moved for what seemed like 10 minutes. When the players did make a move to go back down the tunnel they came back out again. The Queens fans started to drift away into the concourse behind the stand and there was utter disbelief that we had qualified for the final and done it in such a brilliant way. Total strangers with only Queens in common were hugging each other. There was a quiet disbelief until the goals were replayed on the screens above the food outlets. To make matters more surreal someone uttered the words if Rangers got to the final then Queens would be in the UEFA Cup.

A magical day seeing Queens play at Hampden Park, beat an SPL team, score four goals, get to the Scottish Cup final and the potential for qualifying for Europe. This was a day for the real supporters who have followed the team through thick and thin, the big defeat games, the wet away games, the away trips to Clyde, East Fife, Berwick, supporters who had followed Queens throught the 70's, 80's and 90's before the recent years of limited success. If only the final will be as good?

William Johnstone
Dumfries

The highlight of the Queens cup campaign was the tremendous rapport the players had with the fans and vice-versa.

Joining that was the semi-final performance by the man of the tournament Stevie Tosh who wore the No. 8 shirt with distinction, a true professional Queens man.

Ian Spence, Lockerbie

"My wife Daniella is originally from Brisbane, Australia. Her parents Ron and Lindy had arranged a trip over to visit us in April. We had arranged to go on a tour around Scotland, everything was booked and arranged. Then unbelievably Queens managed to get past Dundee with the help of a piece of Stephen Dobbie skill and a wonder goal from Ryan McCann!! Fantastic! Amazing! Just one problem. The pre-arranged trip.

I had to change the end of the tour so that we travelled from Inverary in Argyll to Hampden on the day of the semi-final. I also had to make sure I got my in-laws tickets. Having sorted all this out, Ron and Lindy arrived and we set off around Scotland through the snow and rain of early April! While they were enraptured by the architectural beauty and history of Edinburgh and the stunning landscape of Skye my mind was never far away from the Saturday to come and what would happen at Hampden against Aberdeen. "we will get beat 3 nil" I kept telling

them. "it would be good if we could score though" I said hopefully.

The morning of the day came and we headed south to the national stadium. After the most amazing semi-final ever, Queens had done it. We were in the final. Unbelievable! I asked the Aussies if they had enjoyed it and my father in law said that he had been looking forward to the occasion but was really pleased we had won as he "liked to be surrounded by winners". Surrounded he certainly was, 10,000 ecstatic, slightly shocked Doonhamers celebrated in style. Queens had gained two new Australian fans who would spread the word down under. They made sure they got the live goals commentary for the final and were jumping about in their "Queenslander" home when big Jim Thomson did the unthinkable by equalising against Rangers. They were as disappointed but proud as I was when we didn't quite make it in the end. 'Mon the south!!!"

James Hogg, Dumfries

The semi-final was an incredible game of football. I hadn't seen a game as exciting as that for a long long time. As a neutral it must have been fantastic to watch.

Peter Latchford
Queen of the South FC

It was without doubt the best game I have ever experienced at Queen of the South in the time I have watched them as far back as 1948.

David Rae
Chairman
Queen of the South FC

Was this a dream? Sat in the front room of a house in Bolton watching Soccer Saturday with Jeff Stelling the vidiprinter comes up with Queen of the South 2, Dundee 0 (Ryan McCann) it was then that I realised history was actually in the making, Queens had booked a semi-final spot at Hampden... yes HAMPDEN!

This followed with frantic text messaging to family and friends some of who wanted to know and others who generally didn't care but EVERYONE had to know! I still had memories of the dark days when I was a little younger as I saw Queens fans throwing their season tickets onto the Palmerston pitch in sheer disgust at what was happening to the club, but also the excitement of Fir Park and the Challenge Cup final against Falkirk that I had made as a young Queens fan only managing to get a ticket after speaking to the then chairman Norman Blount, unfortunately I was living abroad in Sweden when Queens finally won the Challenge Cup and the following promotion to the 1st Division but I followed all the action via the internet and managed to get to games when I came back home to Dumfries.

This was amazing Queens were off to Hampden, but I had a holiday booked and wasn't due back until 12th in the early evening so I was really hoping we would manage a Sunday semi-final, however this wasn't to be so I was resigned to receiving texts from a friend at the match and my brother watching on it on TV walking around the town of Carcassonne in the south of France with my Queen's shirt on receiving texts of 1-0 bringing sheer delight to 3-3 bringing absolute devastation to the 4-3 text sending me into such a nervous state I could hardly talk and could certainly not eat anything, then at Carcsassonne airport check in area a text came in... I opened... and it was it! 4-3 we are off to the final!!!

Lets just say that little airport will never see anything of the likes that followed ever again, a Scotsman with Queens top jumping up and down shouting in an ecstatic state of sheer delight with the biggest smile anyone had ever seen! The local French school kids who were checking in looked rather intrigued and the whole check in stood to a stand still for a few moments! Then it was announced why I was so happy! Of course they wouldn't understand!!!

From then on in it was call after call and text after text organising a ticket and travel to the FINAL! I had waited for this day long enough and there was absolutely no chance of me missing out whatever the cost!

Saturday 24th May 2008 I am woken up by the Prodigy's *Voodoo People* it's 6.00am and we (my brother Michael who had travelled from Newport, Wales) have a huge day ahead of us!

Colin Faulds, Bolton

After leaving Hampden and deciding to walk back into Glasgow, we were all in a bit of shock and excitment that our team had made it to the Scottish Cup final. Cars were tailed back a distance and every couple of minutes it seemed to be the same car pulling up next to us. This one car had the music blaring and when I looked it was full of Aberdeen fans. So this time when it pulled alongside us it happened to be a song I liked and my dancing shoes got a grip of me.

Dancing my way along the streets of Glasgow I noticed in front of me a bed mattress lying outside a shop. Well all the excitement of the day told me go and dive on it. With the Aberdeen fans watching from the car and my mates in stitches I took my run up and dived upon it. Little did I know it was absolutely soaking with rain water.

I was totally drenched. My Queens top was stained but when I looked up the Aberdeen fans were in stitches and peeping their horns. Their reaction made my day and to put a smile on their faces after we had just beaten them would have been hard for anybody.

Mind you I never knew rain water was yellow.

Mark Seaton
Annan

I had ticket panic for a few weeks after the Dundee game but Aberdeen beating Celtic essentially ruled out a sell-out at Hampden. Roughly 10,000 Queens fans turned up for our "cup final" against Aberdeen. Kilted and with our semi-final Queens tops, 20 of us took up nearly a whole row at Hampden.

The game itself was unbelievable. 1-1 at half time and the general feeling was that even if we lost from there we'd done ourselves proud. Pessimistic maybe, but we'd lost Dobbie to a leg injury in the first half, and Queens had a history of failing to beat Premier opposition going back longer than I can remember. Pal Stevie offered to go get the pies at half time – he turned up with the pies about 15 minutes into the second half by which time we were 4-3 up! Fortunately he'd seen all the action on the tellies under the stand. We survived a couple of near things in the second half before winning what most neutrals described as one of the most entertaining semi-finals of all time!

Andy Paterson
Houston
Renfrewshire

We took our 7 year old daughter Kenzie up on the train. It was her first football game and on the way she didn't want a scarf or a flag in fact she didn't even know their colours and had to keep asking us what colour Queens were. By the time we got our seats at Hampden she had her flag and her scarf and one of those mad hats with bells. The atmosphere was amazing as she was shouting and screaming her heart out for Queens to get a glorious victory and the best bit was they did it for her and all the way back on the train she was trying to learn Queens songs and shouting about how great they were. We promised her a season ticket for 2008-09 and I think Queens might just have got another fan for life.

Callum Blackley & Rachel Irving
Dumfries

What a rollercoaster cup ride especially the semi-final great enjoyment when we went ahead then hauled back three times and what an atmosphere at the end as the blue and white scarfs and flags were flying high. Well done Queens more of the same next season please.

Stuart Holden,
Dumfries

It was very well known that in the week leading up to the semi-final I was feeling quite nervous. At the meal on the eve of the match at the Crutherland Hotel, the waitress arrived with a package and asked for Paul Burns. When I opened it, the nappies and hankies spilled out! Jamie McQuilken was the instigator.

Paul Burns
Queen of the South FC

The concourse at Central Station is a fantastic place, buzzing with activity, full of life. In my student days, over twenty years ago now, Central was the hub as I followed Queens round the country. Every second week it would be the start of a journey "doon hame" but most other Saturdays it was the departure point for such exotic destinations as Cappielow, Kilbowie, Douglas Park, Boghead, Broomfield, Rugby Park and even Mount Florida, usually setting off with an ill judged degree of optimism on how the day was going to pan out, and returning dejected, more often than not soaked, to ruin my flatmate's Saturday evening with miserable tales of where it all went wrong.

On April 12th at 3pm, I walked, nope floated, through Central with my two sons and hundreds, of blue shirted Queens' fans and it felt magnificent. We strode through the sunny city centre, tops on, scarves out (rather than stuffed down in a pocket) to meet my wife (shopping – boo!), smiling, laughing, greeting fellow fans as we passed, more proud of being a Queens' fan than I've ever previously felt.

Callum, my eldest boy, doesn't like loud noise. He got a bit upset when Tosher scored and we all went mental. "Don't worry", I reassured him, "I doubt we'll score again"! He didn't go to the final.

Matthew, my other son, has been watching Queens regularly over half his life. He's ten now. In that time he's seen us win Division 2, lift the Challenge Cup, lead Division 1 and to top the lot reach the cup final and qualify for Europe. He thinks Queens are great. He thinks we are a big club. He sees no reason why we shouldn't be in the SPL sooner rather than later. He has not travelled from Central Station to Falkirk, got a bus to Alloa, and lost 3-0 with nine men (yet!), or arrived at Firs Park, Falkirk at 2.45 to hear the half time whistle. I hope he appreciated those Hampden games as much as those that have.

Andrew Penn, Dumfries

They shut the whole town down for the day and it will be the same for the final. The gaffer has done a brilliant job. It was a fantastic result and the biggest day of my football career. I must admit I had a tear in my eye when that final whistle blew.

Jim Thomson
Captain
Queen of the South FC

Whilst flying over Dumfries at 20,000 feet-plus around 9.45pm Saturday night we hit turbulence, I'm convinced it was coming from the ground below, and after the performance Saturday I wouldn't be at all surprised. Waking at 3am my dad and I left Westbury for Bournemouth Airport at 3.45am arriving 5am and checked straight in, amazed to find two more scarf wearing Doonhamers in the departure lounge, one from Weymouth and Scott from Southampton. There were also three "Reds" – now there is a coincidence 4-3!!!

6.30am: My first time ever on a jet, a beautifully smooth Ryanair flight landing in the rain at Prestwick at 7.35, catching the train into Glasgow Central where at 9.15, Dad, Scott and I joined the first few Queens fans in the Crystal Palace for breakfast. Then it was a rocking train to Hampden, where were the opposition fans?

10.50: Watched the team coach arrive and disappear into the bowels of Hampden, time for a few picture opportunities then into the ground.

12.15pm – 2.15: What can I say – to quote both the Sportscene and Sky Sports commentators "Unbelievable". As I watched on the concourse monitor at half time Charlie Nicholas spouted off that class and superior fitness would win the day and he was sticking by his pre-match prediction ... guess who looks a right proper Charlie now!!

Have to be honest I screamed just before John Stewart hit the winner (best I don't quote it word for word) along the lines of "just hit it one", he did and the rest is history, though I could have done without the last 30 minutes. Final whistle, I burst into tears and get a smile

from the policewoman in the control booth behind with a mouthed "aww bless"... David Bowie's *Heroes* summed it all up and I don't think I have ever loved hearing *Don't Stop Me Now* any better than on Saturday. Stayed in the ground until we were kicked out then made our way over to Cathkin Park – somewhere I wanted to visit, were there really still terraces with trees growing out of them? – there were. Watched the local game for a while then made our way back to Mount Florida.

3.15: Back to Central Station a quick trip around the shops turned into a series of apologies to Celtic and Rangers fans who wanted to buy us a drink but we couldn't take them up on their offer as I had to drive back from the airport later that evening. Were they glad we knocked out Aberdeen – you bet, I even had little old ladies giving me cuddles – fantastic I couldn't tell you how many but it took us 30 minutes to get from

Central Station to Crystal Palace again.

5.00: After the souvenir hunting, it was fish and chips under the bridge then back on the train to Prestwick, by now we were all feeling it, the travelling, the emotion, and we just could not settle.

6.00: Finally arrived back at Prestwick for a 8.40 flight, only to find it was going to be 9.40, so we killed time watching West Brom vs Watford and just chilling out – met another three Doonhamers going back to Stanstead and we all said we would be back on the 24th.

9.40: Tried to persuade the Ryanair cabin crew to hang my flag and scarf up at the front of the plane, or better still hang it out of the window but they did not seem too keen on the idea, so they were draped over our seats and as we were first on the plane, we let everyone know where we had been including the three Aberdeen fans who by now were looking really glum. All the way home I gazed out of the window as Scotland

met Northern England (bumpy or what – that was you lot in Dumfries!!) onto Manchester and the Midlands then within no time we were banking over Southampton for landing back at Bournemouth. All the way down it looked as though someone had lit a huge celebration cake, with millions of little orange lights glowing back up to me cruising at 33,000 feet. It was beginning to sink in exactly what we had witnessed, now we were discussing with a small amount of doubt in our minds whether we would get a ticket for the 24th.

Midnight plus 5: Arrived home, as I walked in the door got a huge cheer, hugs and smiles all round from my fiancée and stepkids, once again I burst into tears. Cup of tea, a snack and bed, I had been up 21 hours but now was wide awake, until of course I hit the pillow, where I stayed for 11 hours!!!.

Sunday morning: The flag is now hanging out of the bedroom window, people walking past my house to get their Sunday papers or out for a Sunday stroll are giving it some funny looks – I hide behind the curtain laughing. I sit here whilst I am typing this and ponder – I have to go back for the final, will I get tickets? I would not want to take one away from a regular, genuine supporter one who follows week in week out, but logistics, work and my refereeing career don't allow me the luxury of trips north very often, but given the option I'll be back, the flights are booked already.

And as for Europe... France, Spain, Germany, Italy et al... Hey I have a 400 mile head start on the rest of you, easy peasy... bring it on.

Andy Meaden, Westbury, Wiltshire

We come from a land down under[1] where football is called soccer and I follow a team called Collingwood in the AFL, which stands for, Australian Football League. AFL is played on an oval arena with an oval ball and 18 men a side. Incidentally, there is another organisation in Australia called the ABC which most people think stands for the Australian Broadcasting Commission but it really stands for "Anything but Collingwood." When we are among our brothers in arms the term ABC is a compliment because we enjoy underdog status.

The camaraderie is special and that's how we felt at Hampden Park in April 2008. Our daughter Daniella and her husband James Hogg, who live in Dumfries, had secured us tickets for the game and we were feeling right at home sitting in amongst the Queen of the South crowd.

This was the first time in over half a century that Queens had been in the semi-final and the tension was apparent with only a hint of maybe they could do it. James doesn't talk a lot but he felt it was going to be a close game. "Just remember the story I told you of the battle at Bannockburn," was his advice. He had organised a drive round Scotland for us the previous week and we had felt his tension and sense of excitement.

And now at the ground a few minutes before kick off, it was, for us, like being on another planet.

We call famous AFL grounds hallowed turf and it was great to be a member of the Queen's congregation.

The game got underway and while we had watched soccer... I mean football, on TV in OZ, to be watching it live, to be watching the actual field experience, was an incredible first for us. The crowd involvement was electric and infectious. We had been bitten by the QOS (and so was Aberdeen but with a different bite).

The singing of Louis Armstrong's old favourite seemed logical and fitting. Drummer Boy was another new emotion for us and he has a special place in our hearts now.

All the pre-match nerves were a faint memory.

Queen of the South scored. Aberdeen responded. 1 all.

Queen of the South scored. Aberdeen responded 2 all

Queen of the South scored twice more and Aberdeen could only respond with one, so they went home. They were disappointed but no one rubbed their faces in it – lots of dignity in victory.

The hugging and jumping as the Queen of the South fans lost the Scottish cool and reserve seemed wonderful to us – we like to see emotion expressed and we felt part of this, the biggest win ever for Queen of the South.

I like to be surrounded by winners, because when they laugh it's from the heart and belly and their eyes develop a fiery and gentle look...

I like the discipline of the Queen's fans and I love Status Quo singing *Rocking all Over the World*, but the Doonhamers cover version swept me away.

A mighty day, a mighty win and the way the players acknowledged the loyalty of the fans was a great climax and with Davie Rae saying thanks and calling it the most important day in the club's history, makes me feel blessed that I got to be a part of it.

Ron and Lindy Gottlieb
Brisbane, Australia

[1] Hit tune sung by Men at Work – lead singer Colin Hay, born Kilwining, North Ayrshire in 1953, emigrated to Australia when he was nine-years-old – used as the team song when Australia won the America's Cup 1983

I travelled to the semi-final with the Doonhamers Travel Club and was quite confident we'd pull it off. However, I never expected such a rollercoaster of emotions as we experienced that day against Aberdeen. I feared the worst when Dobbie went off injured, but cometh the hour, cometh the man. That man was John Stewart; if ever a man was pumped up to prove a point, it was him. I saw grown men cry that day, many of whom like me have followed Queens through thick and thin (mostly thin!) for many years. We were subdued on the bus on the way home; I think we were all in a state of shock. Things like this just don't happen to Queen of the South, do they? However, we were less subdued later that night! I've lost count of how many times I've watched re-runs of the semi-final. Nothing can quite beat that feeling of elation at the final whistle: we were heading to Hampden again!

Chris McKie, Bebington, Wirral

John Stewart... what a fella. He must, like everybody, have known there were doubts about his ability after one goal in 16 appearances prior to the Scottish Cup semi.

When Dobbie was substituted and replaced by Stewart I turned to a mate and said, 'I can't see us scoring again'. What a revelation he turned out to be.

Harley Freemantle, Dumfries

You couldn't have written a script for a game like that – no one would have believed it. To score the winner in a Hampden semi-final is an unforgettable feeling.

John Stewart
Queen of the South FC

How do I sum up yesterday? Simple answer is that I can't. Following Queens for the last 19 years I have seen some low points, cold Tuesday night humiliation in cup games, and some high points, lifting the Bell's Challenge Cup at Broadwood and being crowned Second Division Champions. But yesterday is the best of the bunch. Queen of the South are in the Scottish Cup final, I'll repeat that QUEEN OF THE SOUTH ARE IN THE SCOTTISH CUP FINAL!

Yesterday was a rollercoaster of emotions, waking at 6am with knots in my stomach, I was more nervous than excited, this wasn't helped by Kenny texting me at 6.30 saying practically the same thing, then Ginge texting half an hour later!! Leaving Dumfries at 8.30 we made our way to Moffat, passing some of the many buses leaving the area, once on the motorway we were met by snow, in April, on cup semi day! The buses and cars that we passed on the way added to the excitement. Arriving in Glasgow we made our way to the stadium in time to see the

team buses arrive, we were stared out by Jimmy Calderwood, and waved to Gordon Chisholm. At 11am the turnstiles opened and we made our way to our seats to soak up the atmosphere, flags were waving, scarves were being held aloft. The players made their way to the pitch to start their warm up and the reaction that we gave them made the hairs on the back of my neck stand on end. Wished Sean all the best before the game started. When the players came out of the tunnel again the reaction was phenomenal and the hairs were once again standing on the back of my neck.

The game itself was a rollercoaster as well, Queens taking the lead four times, and Aberdeen equalising 3 times. As the fourth goal went in, I turned to those around me and said "I'm warning you now, I will cry today!" Queens managed to hold on and after what seemed a forever ending four minutes of injury time, the final whistle went. The Queens crowd erupted!! We were in the final!! Again there was cheering, hugging, flags being waved and scarves everywhere – and yes there were tears, I took some time to myself to soak in what had happened – 19 years and this was the best moment ever of being a Queens fan!! The players, management team, chairman all came over to the corner of Hampden that for yesterday was Dumfries! It was a great experience to savour and words fail me even yet. There were cameras everywhere, many of which taking pictures that will be in today's sports pullouts. I was lucky enough to get Sean's attention again amid the celebrations and gave him a hug!

I woke up this morning wondering if it had indeed happened, maybe yesterday was all a dream and that the game hadn't been played yet. But it had happened! Queens had won! And Queens are in the final. It's now six weeks, 40 days until we will make the journey up the road again to Hampden, where again it will be an emotional rollercoaster as QUEENS ARE IN THE SCOTTISH CUP FINAL!

Ross Fraser, Dumfries

The thing I remember most about the whole cup run, apart from the final of course, was the reaction of the Aberdeen fans after the semi-final.

Not one of them had a bad word to say and as we all saw most if not all of them stayed in the ground at full-time to applaud us on what has to be the most amazing game I have ever seen. I am a Queens fan who now lives in Glasgow and was out after the semi in the pubs around Hampden.

What a laugh me and my friends had as we mingled with Aberdeen fans who didn't seem too fussed that they were out of the cup. They knew they had not played well and seemed genuinely happy for us. In fact the only thing they seemed bothered about was us beating Rangers in the final.

In the past I have had a negative opinion of Aberdeen fans, probably because of incidents occurring when the Old Firm play at Pittodrie. Now I think differently. The way they conducted themselves that day was a tribute to the club they support and they deserve a huge pat on the back and a mention in this book.

Paul Nelson, Glasgow

Saturday 24th May 2008 was an incredible day for Queen of the South Football Club and its fans – for me it was a bittersweet occasion being first and foremost a lifelong Aberdeen fan. Ultimately of course I would have preferred my first love the Dandy Dons to have been at Hampden and beaten our arch enemy Rangers to lift the Scottish Cup for an 8th time, but alas it was not to be as a consequence of the events of Saturday 12th April at Hampden, when the Doonhamers deservedly beat Aberdeen to reach their first Scottish Cup final.

I did not even get to the semi as a prior family arrangement – my mum's 75th birthday party whereby the whole Gardiner clan met up for lunch in St Andrews took precedence. But what a way to be kept in touch with events at the National Stadium (there was no TV in Rufflets Hotel) so my Aberdeen-supporting mates were texting me the score updates – to be honest it was an unbelievably painful way to follow events and one I would not want to go through again. I guess the first reaction on realising the Dons were out was "Thankfully I wasn't there" quickly followed by "Our best chance of getting to a final for years and we lose to a lower league side".

The only small consolation I could take is that the Reds had been beaten by one of my childhood favourites, Queen of the South.

As a child being brought up in the Lake District, live football consisted of periodic visits to Borough Park to see Workington in the old English 4th Division before they were demoted, Brunton Park to see Carlisle United flit between the lower English leagues and Palmerston to see the magnificently named Queen of the

South generally struggle between the old Scottish 1st and 2nd divisions post the 1975 league reconstruction. I always had a soft spot for Queens, owning the old fashioned blue and white 'bar scarf' and developing an affinity with such greats as Allan Ball, Iain McChesney, Jim Coughlin, Peter Dickson, Nobby Clark, Tommy Bryce etc

Memorable trips to Palmerston included the League Cup quarter-final against Rangers in 1975 (a 2-2 draw I think which went into extra time ?) – the ground was rocking and difficult to imagine that the 7500 crowd could have been more than doubled for a Scottish Cup tie against the same opponents around the same time. Other games in a dire relegation season (1978-9) included Ayr United (absolutely freezing cold) and Dundee and later on in another relegation season (1982) against champions Motherwell right at the end where there were only 500 people there but my brother Neil and I, now living in Edinburgh had got the bus down to Dumfries for the match and managed to get ourselves into the bar in the main

stand and served pints of lager shandy at the ages of 16 and 14 respectively !!

As a family we also watched Queens play some away games in the Central Belt in the early 80s including a miserably wet day in Cowdenbeath in 1982 where our homemade QOS banner ended up very tatty and paint stained by the end of the match after a torrential downpour on the open terracing at Central Park.

In more recent years I have seen Queens play the Dandy Dons in the two Scottish Cup matches and League Cup game in this millenium. The 0-0 draw in front of a near 6,000 crowd at Palmerston brought back happy memories of old times for me and what the atmosphere of the Scottish Cup was all about. Chats in the boardroom at the Pittodrie replay with the Queens directors impressed upon me that the club was in good hands and was going the correct way as did a chat with Allan Ball in the Palmerston boardroom at the League Cup game the following season

And so after all this history, later on in the evening of the fateful semi-final defeat and after a few medicinal drinks

I agreed with my brothers that we would go to the cup final and support Queens whoever they were to play – knowing inevitably it would be the undesirables from Govan !!

Cup final day was just fantastic – our party of 4 were Queens fans for the day (and in my brother Neil and my case for many years before that) and enjoyed a good lunch in di Maggio's before heading to the exec lounges at Hampden and take our seats in the South Stand along side the 15000+ Doonhamers.

Not much can be said about the game that hasn't been said already – after a slow first half Queens came to life after the break and the feeling of elation as the goals went in at the end housing the Dumfries contingent was just magic – if only they had managed to get a 3rd goal.

The Queens support on the day was brilliant – outsinging the muted Rangers contingent for large periods of the game and even in defeat they stood behind their team – a credit to the club, the town and south-west Scotland

For me it was back to Aberdeen to reflect on a season of what might have been for the Dons, but also to feel immense pride in the performance of our conquerors in the cup final – for that day I was proud once more to be a Queen of the South fan.

All the best for 2008-09 and the Doonhamers Euro run – hopefully the support get to enjoy a good few trips (just like I did with the Dons in Madrid and Munich last season) and hopefully Aberdeen can attempt to get some revenge for the semi-defeat in the SPL in season 2009-10.

Jock Gardiner
Aberdeen

I had a ticket for the semi-final but with my wife feeling that the new baby was close to being born was required to be near to our new home in Gosforth. I managed to get down to the pub to see the "wonder game" against Aberdeen and then back home. That night the waters broke and Poppy Sutherland Carlaw was born, after a 24 hour epic, on the 14th April. Enough brownie points had been earned through missing the game and having a centre stand seat for the birth, to get to the final!!

Ken Carlaw
Gosforth

When Aberdeen beat Celtic, I was almost disappointed – yes, we'd get a bigger than normal crowd, it would be on Sky, we would get national exposure, bloody hell, we even have a better chance of making it to the final, but I really wanted a full house. Still, you can't get everything, and I'm still going to see Queens at Hampden, and that was the most important thing.

Who could ever have dreamed that one day, Queen of the South would contest a Scottish Cup final And so I felt completely at ease before the semi-final – give our all, keep it tight early doors, hit them on the break, nick it one-nil, keep it respectable – all the footballing clichés were being mentioned, but really it was all about being there.

But that soon changed when Tosher scored, and when Burnsy scored, and when Sean scored and when John Stewart scored – every time it looked like the form book was flying back in the window, we threw it back out again, and it became a winnable match – it was the daftest 15 minutes of football anyone has probably ever seen, but it ended with us being 4-3 up, and for the next 30 minutes just being there wasn't enough. We deserved to win this game, and so it was that 10,000 Doonhamers prayers came true and we did. I'll never forget the feeling when the full-time whistle went, and I didn't think I'd ever feel any better again.

Mark McMinn

Dumfries

Probably the best day of my fourteen year old life by far. The atmosphere, the build up and of course the final whistle it just couldn't be put into words. I don't think I even used my seat on the bus all the way there because of the excitement and nerves and when we reach the pub it was amazing. Queens fans at one end and Aberdeen fans at the other side singing for a few hours solid before everyone started to make their way to Hampden.

Never seen the hairs on my arms stick up so far, I was in shock with so much excitement at seeing my team come out for the warm up. The crowd just lifted and the stand was rocking with songs. Then as the kick off started to approach I got that nervous feeling again thinking that in 90 minutes time we could be in the final of the Scottish Cup and also have our chance at European football next season. It was probably the most entertaining game of football I had ever seen my team play, end to end and Aberdeen certainly made it hard for us 'Doonhamers' but in the end we had the final burst of effort and I still wonder how big Sean O'Connor managed to jump on John Stewart's shoulders after he scored the winning goal.

Liam Cullen, Dumfries

I'm aged 41 and been a Palmerston regular since 1975/76. My dad is 67 and started taking me at that time. My brother's 31 and been following Queens for around maybe 20 years. Between the 3 of us that's around 139 years of age with 84 years following Queens. By the end of the day each one of us declared that this was the BEST day of our lives. That says it all. A really special day, special match and special result.

By the time the 3rd and 4th goals went in we are going off our heads. At one point I was celebrating so much I was almost standing on my brothers head from above. I was pushing down on him so hard he could hardly get up (and he's bigger than me). At the end of the game there were tears, mental cheers, dancing and cries and statements of disbelief (I reckon I repeated the sentence of "I don't believe it, I can't believe it at least 50 times in the 10 minutes after the final whistle). Amazingly the bus was fairly quiet on the way back down, as we were all in shock and many were stunned into silence. When we got back to Locharbriggs and Dumfries it seemed like we were heroes coming back from the war as people looked out of their houses to give us a wave.

For days afterwards we were all getting emotional every time we thought about and re-lived the match. It was like living in a surreal world. When TV advertised the cup final due on the very last day of the season we didn't know who we'd be playing but WE were there and possibly in Europe. We were all overcome with emotion for days.

Stuart Rae, Dumfries

The definition of a stalker in a rather handy dictionary I have nearby is one who stalks game. For stalk it's to follow stealthily. Now my friends and I could never quite justify an appearance in court for our stalking capabilities but purely by accident – this is important to stress – we got the chance to perfect those skills one glorious day in Glasgow.

Picture the scene. A titanic battle had just ensued in Hampden. Two mighty teams, partial to a few charitable donations at the back, had slogged it out. One was led by a former Black Cat, the other by a manager whose visage matched the national flag of the country where he spent most of his playing career. By the end of the match Mr Calderwood's face had gone through three separate colours – orange, red and then ashen white (or maybe peach in his case) when he realised the mighty Queens had dumped his lot out 4-3.

Buzzing on pure adrenalin, it was never our intention to head back home. Instead, off we trooped, city centre bound. Personally, I was looking forward to meeting up with an old pal, Crazy Dave (sorry Davie), an Aberdeen fan who had the guts and, he'll say, boyish good looks to deflect any Queens' supporter's good-natured banter. The meeting point was the Auctioneers pub, for no other reason than in our increasingly jolly state we remembered it had a big screen TV to watch whatever English match was on later that day. Davie promptly arrived looking sheepish – I had to do it – and withstood all the levity thrown his way. He even went so far as agreeing to be draped in a Queens' scarf. You are a God among Dons Davie.

With our squad now complete we headed off to our next stop, Republic Bier Halle, where we had agreed to meet the triumphant Queens' players. Pause. I must confess that last statement may not be entirely true, okay not at all true – remember this is a story about stealthily following game. But back to the hunt, where to our surprise a large contingent of the team was present and correct celebrating, seemingly having swapped their strips for matching grey jumpers. Stephen Dobbie went another way – pin stripe suit, black shirt, it's a good thing he can score goals.

Excitement ensued, Davie tried to hide from what he knew was coming and pictures were posed. The players were in fine form and had smiles as wide as can be, especially when introduced one by one to the Crazy pal. It was important you see that he was made to congratulate each one, both because it would help him grow as a person and of course for our amusement. An hour later they headed out, drifting away to their next location. But we were not finished with what – 15 drinks down the road – can only be described as giddy hero worship. So a plan was hatched.

Conscripting my brother – a non-football fan who begrudgingly admitted at Hampden with two minutes to go as Queens hung on to their final dream that it was "quite exciting" – we set him off in pursuit, to stalk or to follow stealthily. Amongst full Glasgow nightlife, he dived behind lampposts, hurdled benches and acted nonchalantly as he kept his prey in sight. Spy? He was a moody, greying James Bond! Location confirmed he came back to headquarters to report. Our next destination agreed we set off while perfecting our surprised "Oh fancy banging into you again" faces as we went.

I've never been one for remembering bar names – it's hard to focus sometimes – but entering that licensed premises our agreed expressions were put into practice.

Whatever the bar was called – I will have been told by now – it managed to satisfy our thirst to mingle with the team who had given so much to everyone hours before.

For my girlfriend it was the chance to confirm through a gentle stroke, or several, (put the man down) that Stephen Dobbie's facial stubble is "Oh, so soft." He kept on coming back to chat.

But for us all it was a chance to thank the players who were class that night to us mere supporters and class on the pitch earlier that day. At Hampden, Gods among men.

Now the time we met Eric Paton and the boys at 11 pm in Chester in 2004 is another story all together. Let's just say: 'John Travolta, Gary Wood wants a dance off.'

Alan Hall, Dumfries

Like weary prizefighters. Arms aloft, mouths gaping, no sound coming out, nothing left in the tank. The emotional drainage of the previous twelve minutes had taken its toll. That – and the knowledge that already three times we had celebrated, that three times we'd cursed our inability to hold on to the lead. And the knowledge absorbed it seemed while still in the womb – that the sole purpose of football is to kick you in the teeth when you are up.

And we were being asked to get our hopes up one more time. Yeah good one Queens.

In a stadium with more than 20,000 other people the next thirty minutes couldn't have felt more personal. Here was me, and here was the game being played out in front of me which I was utterly, utterly wired to. For those thirty minutes nobody and nothing else mattered. This, after twenty-two years, was the culmination of the emotional investment I'd put into the team: the boyhood dreams, the teenage realisation that they were never going to come true. Even (sometimes I've thought it) the fact that I'd be less of a pessimist about life in general if it wasn't for spending my formative years watching Queen of the South in the 1990s. My heart was pounding, I felt sick to the stomach. I cried at least twice before the game had even finished. Not fun this, more a perverted, horrible masochism.

We stood there for ages after the final whistle, long after the players had made their way down the tunnel. I wanted to drink in every last drop, for the moment never to end. More than anything I was in shock, I couldn't believe it. (How many times did I use the phrase that day?)

The years of misery – the years when the directors picked the team –the years of five, six, seven goal defeats – all saved up and cashed in for a prize better than any I ever imagined for Queens.

Aided by a pint or two the initial shock subsided over the course of the afternoon. What followed was the biggest party ever. Beer, whisky, vodka, bottles of champagne being passed around the bar, congratulatory hands offered everywhere. I wanted to hug everyone. So big were our grins, and so repeated were the cantbelieveits and amazings coming from our mouths that some people thought we were all on drugs. We toasted the players, we toasted the manager, we toasted each other. And after all these years – Willie – yes we toasted him too.

It went on long into the night. I think it was one of the happiest days of my life. Really. And all evening, just a few feet away from me were some of my best friends, guys I had been going to watch Queens with for years, having one of the happiest days of theirs.

Two months on and still a shiver up my spine, a smile on my face, a tear in my eye as I write about it. Brilliant, so brilliant.

Walt Adamson, Glasgow

QUEENS DEL SOL

Marbella, April 2008

We had a re-arranged league match against Partick in the midweek after the semi-final against Aberdeen. Chis had decided to play some of the fringe players that night and during the warm up Jamie MacDonald was firing some shots into Stephen Grindlay.

The guy next to me shouted over to Jamie asking if he "wisnae startin' the night?" to which Jamie replied, "naw the gaffers dropped me for letting in three on Saturday."

Kenny Scott
Dumfries

The lengthy build up was obviously a problem for Gordon Chisholm and the team with the lack of match practice. However, I really enjoyed the time looking forward to the big game. From the ticket sales to seeing the shops and houses sporting Queens colours and the extensive media coverage, it was a time to enjoy and savour. (Also, we had a UEFA Cup spot in the bag already!).

The 24th May became more than just a football match – it was a major event for Dumfries and the surrounding area. Working in Dumfries on the day before the final it was great to see the merchandise sellers (official and unofficial) doing a roaring trade. Almost everyone in town proudly wore the colours (hats, scarves or flags as the saying goes). I walked home that afternoon sensing the feelgood atmosphere in the streets and daring to dream of what was to come at Hampden the following afternoon.

Gordon Harper
Dumfries

YER HAME TEAM'S YER AIN TEAM

Cup final week in Dumfries

Over the years, Queens fans have become used to anonymity. The media attention that came the way of the New Bazaar Doonhamers in the latter stages of the cup run therefore came as quite a shock. Our first encounter with the press was the week before the quarter-final v Dundee when the Sun was looking for some quirky stories. Fitting the bill were the NBD guys with their wooden rattles who duly dominated the front page of the 'Sun's Saturday Sports Supplement'. We thought that calm had returned thereafter but the decision to wear Davie Rae wigs and masks to the final away game of the season (v Dunfermline) again propelled us to the fore. Now we were being described in a selection of newspapers as 'wacky'. We thought this was going a bit too far – Is it fair to describe middle aged men wearing wigs, masks and wielding 1950's style rattles as wacky?... Probably!

The New Bazaar became very busy in the week before the final and NBD members were filmed singing, rattling and chatting by crews from the BBC, GMTV and Sky. Some of us were even interviewed and my brief contribution resulted in me being mocked for days by friends and strangers. When asked about Queens chances, I seemed to say that Queens were better than Rangers. In fact my response in full was "Queens have a good chance. Rangers struggled in previous rounds against Partick Thistle and St. Johnstone and we are as good as they are and probably better!" They only used the last part! Still, by cup final day we were at our informed, incisive and witty best when interviewed live for BBC Radio. By the way did anyone actually hear Willie Johnstone's live link at 9.10 on Saturday 24th May? Did anyone record it?

Jim Harkness
Dumfries

I have been following Queens for about 25 years and have never seen anything like this during that time, it is a fantastic achievement for the club to reach the Scottish Cup final and it's great to see the town and club in the newspapers and on national TV. I will be going to the game with my father, my son Jamie who is only 6 and 2 of my mates. The Queens fans are going to have a great day out at Hampden and here's hoping they beat Rangers and bring the cup back to Dumfries!

Mark Ovens
Annandale Insurance
Dumfries

Margaret Hanlon has run this family business for over 25 years. She has been in the trade for 45 years and has seen many faces come and go, but many have never changed. Margaret and all her customers are getting excited about the forthcoming match. She and her family were brought up in Glencaple, hence a soft spot for Sean O'Connor, who is due to marry a local Glencaple lass Jennifer Houliston (grand-daughter of the great Billy Houliston – the only man fully capped for Scotland while playing for Queens)

Kate Clark
Jaqueline's Hairdressers
Dumfries

It was wonderful to see the smile on my dad's face when he saw my window display, I don't think he ever thought a beauty salon would do it. He is a Queens supporter but because of illness he doesn't go to matches anymore. I wish them all the best of luck and I hope all their dreams come true.

Ineke Thomson
Beautified Salon
Dumfries

What an event for the whole town. Blue & white in shops and good luck messages everywhere, even on peoples roofs. TV and media were everywhere. The New Bazaar Doonhamers were featured on GMTV, Sky Sports, STV, Reporting Scotland and Radio Scotland. Jim Harkness, Brian Kelly, Robbie Purdie and Colin Hamilton all became media stars as spokespersons for the group and were almost able to command a fee for autographs by the weekend of the final.

Stuart Rae, Dumfries

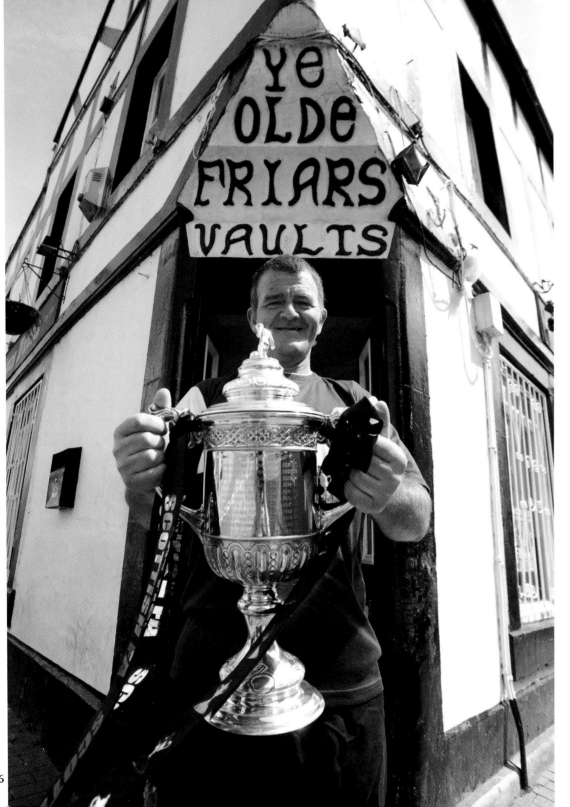

This Saturday May 24 2008 has already gone down in history in the Scottish town of Dumfries, home to football team Queen of the South. For the first time in their 89-year history, they have reached the Scottish Cup final.

They will take to the Hampden turf against a Rangers side who were last week swaggering towards an unprecedented and much vaunted quadruple, but who now appear to be staggering towards the season end finale. Having lost to Aberdeen on Thursday, the SPL title has been retained by Celtic. On Saturday they are up against a team whose own league season finished four weeks previous.

As a Queen of the South fan, I have a vested interest in the final stages of this season, and I have to say, it is proving to be most enjoyable.

A brief history may be beneficial to those who are not fully versed in the many honours achieved by the south west Scotland club. Don't worry however, it won't take up too much of your time. Founded in 1919, when 3 clubs in the town merged to form Queen of the South United. The United was dropped over the years, presumably as their moniker was a mouthful as it was. Their illustrious list of honours can be counted on one hand, winning two Division 2 championships as well as a Challenge Cup, or Mickey Mouse Cup, as it's affectionately known.

When this record is stacked up against the Rangers one then you may ask, why bother turning up? But we all know why – because upsets can happen. This is seen as a once in a lifetime occasion for all Queens fans, and it is one which will be cherished by many all the way to the grave.

Queen of the South, nicknamed the Doonhamers, proved in the semi-final against Aberdeen that they are no pushovers, battling through 4-3 against the SPL side in what is the highest scoring semi ever in the world's oldest club cup competition. As well as being the highest scoring it is widely thought of as being the most entertaining football spectacle for many a year. SFA President, Gordon Smith described the match as, "one of the greatest matches we have seen in the Scottish Cup."

We all remember Gretna's run in the Scottish Cup in 2006, where they fell at the last hurdle against Hearts, and the headlines portrayed the romance of plucky little Gretna, but the headlines glossed over the facts that Gretna at the time were paying SPL wages to SPL players. In reality it wasn't a shock that

they proceeded so far in the competition.

This season, there are shock troops in operation, and they take on the guise of Queen of the South. They are truly living the dream, and all whilst remaining clear of debt to the banks, and with a skeletal playing staff of only 20.

I was lucky enough to be present the last time we won significant silverware in 2001, when the Division Two championship was claimed, and I remember thinking at the time, that I probably wouldn't see another day like this for many a year. It appears I have been blessed as I head to Hampden on Saturday, to witness what will be a wonderful occasion; win, lose or draw.

You see, to me this goes further than just a football game. Queens fans have never been blessed with good fortune.

To reach the final is the equivalent of Westmeath reaching the All Ireland final. To win would compare to London taking Sam home to England.

This will have an impact on real people. Punters who refuse to follow their team through the medium of TV, and through the newspapers. Anyone can do that. Following your home team through your life teaches you great lessons in life – mainly how to deal and cope with disappointment, but when the highs come along they are surely more euphoric than notching up your 32nd Scottish Cup win, as in Rangers' case should they win on Saturday.

Locally within Dumfries a campaign was started a number of years ago. Their tag line being "yer hame team's, yer ain team." It was set up to lure the locals to come back to Palmerston Park, Queens' home ground, and reduce the number of Old Firm fans who headed in their droves 80 miles north to watch their easily accessible heroes win another game 4-0. Or those who choose to watch the vacuous chat from expert pundits on a live scoreboard beamed live into their homes.

Come Saturday it will be refreshing, as the droves will be following their home team, where every generation will be represented. My 81 year old father and 4 year old nephew being prime examples.

Whatever the outcome, it will be a day to remember for all. Prediction? Well , elation, for the very fact of being there. Every true sports fan should get the chance to experience an occasion like this. The scoreline, irrelevant. I lie, of course. 1-0 to Queens would suit me, just fine!

Martin McGarva Smith, Dublin

A mass exodus will take place tomorrow as Queen of the South embark on their biggest day.

Fans have been plotting their trip to the cup final with military precision since the semi-final victory over Aberdeen on April 12.

And hope springs eternal among the thousands of Queens fans, certain they have what it takes to emerge victorious in the battle with Rangers.

The Blue Army have put their faith in a manager, a chairman and 11 players who will pull on the famous blue and white of Queen of the South – a band of brothers united in pursuit of the Scottish Cup.

At the club's Palmerston headquarters, fans snapped up the small allocation of just 15,476 tickets within days of them going on sale. Dumfries businesses, eager to show their colours, have kitted out windows and doorways with good luck messages, while a victory parade the day after the final will ensure a heroes' welcome for Gordon Chisholm's troops.

And if Chisholm can guide his side to the win... never in the field of sporting contest will so much have been owed by so many to so few.

As Rangers hectic schedule catches up with them, there are few who believe for sure that the cup will stay in Scotland's second city.

With Dobbie, Stewart and O'Connor providing the firepower up front, Thomson, Aitken and MacDonald marshalling the rearguard and Burns and McQuilken bursting down the flanks – Queens are a force to be reckoned with.

For the Blue Army, it truly is the day of days.

Let it be their finest hour.

Harley Freemantle, Dumfries Courier

Basically, Queen of the South is in my blood. My grandfather was a director of the club, my granny helped in the pie and Bovril stall and my dad wrote a club history and went on to become a director and then chairman of the club. From an early age, I can remember following in the family tradition and cheering on the Queens. The 70's and 80's saw some great players Allan Ball, Tommy Bryce and Iain McChesney to name a few. But they also saw tough times. I remember standing on the terracing in driving rain at Meadowbank Thistle one November Saturday afternoon in the late 80's and wondering, am I mad?

I never thought I'd see Queens at Hampden in a Scottish Cup final. It was just a daft dream but unbelievably it has come true, thanks to a visionary chairman, a fantastic manager and a great squad of players combining experience and youth. Whatever happens on Saturday, after this remarkable cup campaign and the extraordinary Aberdeen game, they will forever be legends.

Stephen Jardine
Scottish Television presenter

CHAPTER 6
RANGERS

Today's the day the Teddy Bears have their cup nicked!

QUEEN OF THE SOUTH 2, RANGERS 3

SATURDAY 24 MAY 2008
SCOTTISH CUP FINAL
Hampden Park
QUEENS SCORERS: **Tosh 50, Thomson 53**
Attendance: **48,821**

QUEEN OF THE SOUTH

1	MacDonald
2	McCann (**17** Robertson, 86)
3	Harris
4	MacFarlane
5	Aitken
6	Thomson
7	McQuilken (**14** Stewart, 76)
8	Tosh
9	O'Connor
10	Dobbie (**15** O'Neill, 82)
11	Burns

SUBS NOT USED:

12	Grindlay
16	Paton

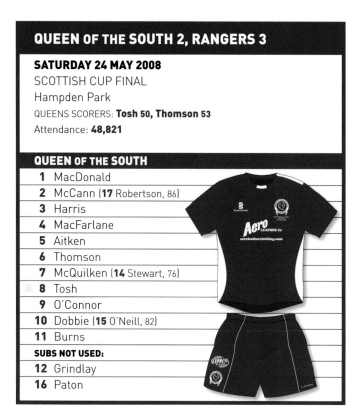

I'm not a great singer at the football. In fact I'm not a great singer at all, but after Thomson's header, the compulsion to join in the chorus of "You're not singing anymore" was overpowering.

The Rangers fans around and above us looked bewildered and during a fifteen minute spell of gross dereliction of duty, Derry's walls did indeed have to go undefended.

No-one who sang that song that day will forget it. Ever.

Geoff Leonard, Dumfries

Cup final day arrived (why is it always sunny on cup final day?) and the road to Hampden got off to a great start as the feelgood factor of the previous day continued. Members of the Dumfries public, young and old, stood at the roadside waving off the hundred of cars and buses through Locharbriggs and passing Amisfield wishing the Queens good luck.

The game itself, as did the semi-final, exceeded my expectations and my favourite memory is the chorus of "You're not singing anymore" directed at the Rangers support as Queens roared back from a two-goal deficit and for a few minutes looked as if they would be crowned Scottish Cup winners 2008!

Gordon Harper
Dumfries

Leaving Dumfries on cup final morning and seeing all the townsfolk decked in blue and white really brought it home to me the magnitude of the team's achievement.

Ian Black
Queen of the South FC

Fitba' Flashback
Palmerston, Queens v Rangers:
(Ah wis a wean back then)
They thocht it wuid be easy,
The mighty Rangers men –
But Big Jim in the goalmooth
Did a gracefu' pirouette
And a nifty wee backheeler –
And the ba' wis in the net.
Jim Patterson, a Queens man –
Misca' him if ye daur,
Tho whyles they shouted "cairthorse"
And whyles they shouted waur –
Yit skills he hud a-plenty
And agility as well
And that day he wis shair-fuited
As an African gazelle.
Ye micht say Ah wis dreamin,
Ye micht say Ah wis blind,
And whit the final score wis
In truth Ah cannae mind,
But yin thing Ah remember,
Ah kin see it clear as day –
Big Jim did a backheeler
And he pit the ba' away.
We'll be gaithered roun Saint Peter
When oor race doon here is run
And the crack will be o' oor guid deeds
And some we hivnae done.
But the Saint will treat us kindly
(And a Queens top he'll hiv on)
And he'll stroke his beard and reminisce:
"Man, that wis some goal yon!"
                    Donald Adamson, Dalbeattie

I am very privileged and feel humbled to have been part of Queen of the South's first ever appearance in a major cup final.

                    John Kerr
                    Queen of the South FC

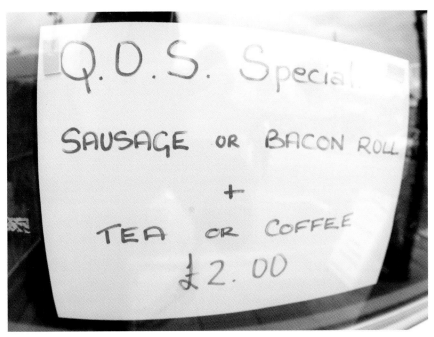

The big day arrived and with mounting excitement the Doonhamers Travel Club buses filled up rapidly in the old Tesco car park adjacent to Palmerston. Even Border TV (who are usually Carlisle Utd orientated) sent a cameraman to see the fans off. Sticking to the route 'advised' by Strathclyde's polis we entered the east end of No Mean City, passing by Celtic Park where wreaths still lay in memory of Bhoys legend Tommy Burns. Turning left we passed another famous old ground – Shawfield – once the home of Clyde now decanted to Broadwood, near Cumbernauld where the Bully Wee struggle to get the locals to support them.

Parking in Polmadie Road the blue and white army set off on a fairly long walk to the pre-booked hostelry The Beechwood. On arrival we were met by the manageress who was vetting that we were, indeed, bona fide Travel Club members and in we piled. To our surprise the pub was already quite full and owing to three bar staff not turning up for their shift (allegedly) the ones on duty were run off their feet. It took 25 minutes to get the 5 pints I needed for myself and my mates and we eventually settled down at a table. However, more and more Queens fans poured in, and despite the Travel Club Committee members helping out on the door the manageress called in two bouncers to deal with the chaotic scene. It was now virtually impossible to get served but it was discovered that through the back was a function room with bar, so in we went. Others followed and for a little while we drank in peace. But that was shattered when the redoubtable manageress suddenly appeared and roared "Aw the Travel Club members in here please leave now". Seemingly the pub had booked in another bus from Dumfries to use the function room and as one lot left the other Doonhamers came in. Brassing it out three of us sat still and no-one noticed/bothered so up to the bar I went. This was situated in the corner up a little stair and was the size of a normal living room with seats around the walls. Sorry sir, says the barmaid – sit down and when it's your turn come up to the bar. Shaking the heid I went back to tell my, by now, thirsty mates who laughed out loud at this latest scenario. But hold on – suddenly the pub came up with another plan – instead of waiting until you were called a guy appeared with a stamper and, if you wanted any bevvy, stamped your wrist (it reminded me of a pass-out at the jigging many years ago). This was the last straw and we exited the dark dingy function room back to the much brighter main bar. Many, many fans were still trying their luck to get in but as time went on things eventually settled down and, in the end we did manage to get a wee swally before setting off to Hampden.

Bruce L. Wright, Dumfries

"We are the people" rang out from the stands now and again and one guy I saw had got it printed on the back of his Rangers top. Many don't like this stuff, but in his case it was helpful as species identification was no formality.

However, special mention must go to the Queens fan who beautifully undermined the groundless arrogance of the slogan with his own witty, self deprecating version.

Accompanying a photo of Dumfries' best known landmark, the legend on his T-shirt simply read "We Are The Steeple".

Geoff Leonard
Dumfries

The cup final against Rangers was the first Queens game that I took my daughter to.

This was history repeating itself in some small way as the first game that my dad took me to when I was eight years old was also against Rangers in October 1962 at Palmerston which Queens lost 4-0.

My abiding memory of that game was watching a big Jim Baxter volley sail over the Portland Drive roof during the pre-match warm up.

My abiding memory of the cup final will be big Jim Thomson's header hitting the back of the net to make the score 2-2 and the celebrations that followed.

Robin Thomson
Blanefield

My partner is a Dumfries lass and through her Uncle John I got interested in Queens and adopted them as my Scottish team. Due to being a season ticket holder at Walsall, visits were few and far between, we saw the 3-0 win over Morton as Queens won promotion, victory in the Challenge Cup over Brechin at Broadwood, a draw against Airdrie and the never to be forgotten semi-final win over Aberdeen. This meant that I was defending an unbeaten run going into the final.

We arrived in Eastriggs on Friday night to meet our family and friends from Carlisle and Australia. John, nearing 60, was like a teenager. He had bought everything, shirts, scarves, flags, hats and couldn't pass the ground or the shop without buying something! The best was yet to come as he showed us our transport to Hampden the following day a Hummer Limo – awesome!

Heads were turned all the way to Glasgow as we had a glass or two to lubricate our throats whilst waving to all the Queens fans on the road. On the outskirts of Glasgow we ran out of beer and pulled up outside a Spar Shop to top up supplies!

As an Englishman I must confess to being disappointed with Hampden, maybe it is different for internationals but it's not the cauldron I expected.

Having been a referee for over 10 years I was disappointed to see how the Old Firm get decisions go for them first hand, Rangers already in front got away with murder as big Sean gets a two handed push in the back

in the box, a nailed on penalty anywhere else but in front of the Rangers fans at Hampden.

Two down at half time Queens were on the ropes but rallied magnificently to level for a few minutes. The dream was alive but the next goal went the wrong way as Queens lack of match fitness proved costly. Rangers had their expected win but were pushed all the way by a gutsy Queens side whose reward is a place in the UEFA Cup next season.

The Sunday saw us at Palmerston to pay tribute to the lads before heading back down the M6 – Queens scarf flying proudly.

See you in Europe – we will be there!

Steve Davies, South Derbyshire

Originally from Dumfries, but having lived down south for 16 years finding any coverage of Queens is difficult to say the least. Prior to this spring, if you had mentioned football to my 6-year old daughter Ellen, she would have talked about the likes of Chelsea and Man U but never her father's boyhood favourites. Even I was beginning to forget they existed.

Then, one evening in March, a tiny news report popped up on TV, telling of McCann's 84th minute winner to put Queens in the semi-final against Aberdeen – I had to go!

I knew tickets would be difficult to come by but remembered my folks had bought me a share in the club 15 years ago. I looked at the Queens website and could see that this may help me get a brief. I contacted the office to obtain my share number only to be told by the club's accountant " I was dead!" I kid you not.

Apparently, they had tried for years to trace me but only had the address seven previous to my current one. They had even put a post on the club forum asking my whereabouts, to which someone replied "I believe he's dead". After guaranteeing I was alive and well, I got my share number and before long tickets were in hand for the semi-final.

What a day! We arrived in Glasgow after a very early start and met up with some old school friends via the internet to watch the most sensational match ever before returning home very late. All of the in between stuff was just HALLUCINO-GENIC. I'm still not sure if any of it really happened! I remember calling my brother in Vancouver (big Queen's fan) and awoke him from his sleep with the result – now what a way to be woken up!

Queens were going to the final. I was going to the final and Ellen was going to the final too. No matter what, we were going and so we did! She loved every minute of the day and so did I. It was magical, it was memorable and it was all about Queens, me and her. She loved the fact that nearly every form of transport was used: car – bus – plane – bus – train and the reverse to get home! It was crazy, non-stop and the best football experience of my life.

Ellen bought the biggest flag possible with her pocket money and proceeded to take out fans from both clubs swinging it around on our walk to Hampden. Inside the ground, she was terrified at first. We grabbed a drink when we arrived and then walked over towards our seats. As she took her first look towards the pitch and all the fans, her little jaw dropped. It was only days later that she told me she was really frightened but 'in a good way', oh to feel that moment again as an adult! We had a great time. I was among my neighbours and friends again from years ago and it felt great.

The match result was not one of loss for me but just part of a memory for life. Ellen and I shared moments that day we will never forget. She told me she was embarrassed when Daddy was screaming 'like a girl' but loved it 'when I held her up like Simba in The Lion King' just after Queens equaliser.

Now Queens are back in my life and certainly in Ellen's. The Surrey-born 6-year old sings no longer of Chelsea, Newcastle or Man U. Instead, she turns to me now and again and sings 'NA-NA-NA-NA NA-NA-NA-NA QUEENS!'

Great. Unforgettable. Emotional.

Craig Hodgson
Surrey

With the banner in the back window and the Queens club logo stuck to side windows, Queens scarves flying from the windows we headed from Bolton to Dumfries, I had been looking forward to this game for weeks and now we are only a matter of hours from a Scottish Cup final the excitement was building, on our way up the M6 we had people wishing us well with thumbs up and big smiles as they passed us and then it was to Hampden!

The sheer numbers of Queens fans there made me step back and the noise we all created was exceptional but the moment I will never ever forget was when Jim Thomson rose up and brilliantly headed the ball into the back of the net it was 2-2 we had come back from 2-0 we could actually win this...I must admit I was struggling to take it all in but then Rangers had to try and spoil a perfect day by scoring their 3rd which ended up being the winner.

However this day will live with me for the rest of my life 15,000 Queens fans singing, 11 Queens players playing their heart out, and a truly amazing drive back down the M6 knowing we had just been a part of history!

Colin Faulds, Bolton

For the final versus Rangers, Fiona is into making greeting cards and books – she made one for the semi and posted it to Palmerston. She made another one for the final and through a friend it was arranged to hand the book to Davie Rae on cup final day at Hampden. Fiona also got her photo taken with the provost at Hampden, getting a "team photo" on the steps at the stadium.

Once we got into Hampden seeing almost 16,000 Queens fans – superb – said same Queens fans all singing "your no singing anymore" to the Rangers fans.

The feeling at the end of the game was very strange – although we lost the game, I wasn't that disappointed – it felt like a victory. We had played for half the game against the 2nd best team in the country and they had only managed to beat us by one goal.

Derek and Fiona Kirkpatrick
Peterhead

Chris Brotherson and I go on a 9-day golfing trip to Ireland at the same time every year with a squad of lads. Sods law dictated that the cup final fell on the second day of our tour.

This meant us flying to Cork for the first day's golf and of course the mandatory first night on the sauce. When Queens won the semi we had to book flights back to Prestwick on the Saturday morning, then back out to re-join the tour on the Sunday morning.

It all sounded okay in theory but after getting to bed at about 4am on the Friday night we then had to get up at 7.30 to get

a taxi from our hotel to Dungarvan town centre. From there we got a bus to Cork town centre. Another bus from there got us to the airport. We looked a right pair in our Queens tops amongst the 10,000 or so who were flying out for the Munster rugby final!

Horror struck at the airport when we realised our flight was seriously delayed and to top things off the drunken Chris had left his mobile phone in the earlier taxi.

We eventually got into Prestwick just before 2pm and after a bolt to the car and a very rapid drive up the road we

eventually got into Hampden with about 10 minutes to spare!

However, it was all worthwhile considering the performance and it was definitely not an occasion to be missed.

Rules of the golf tour dictated that we still had to stay out on the sauce until after midnight so as not to gain advantage over the remaining touring golfers the next day. It was a long slog, especially having to get up again at 5am to begin the exact same reverse journey back to tour. Needless to say the golfing performance was not of the highest order!

David Balmanno, Dumfries

Having been born and brought up in Aberdeen I am a Dons supporter but when I met my husband in 1983 I also began to follow the fortunes of Queen of the South.

Over the last 25 years our teams have only met twice in cup ties with the Dons winning both times, however when the Scottish Cup 2007/08 began in November we could never have imagined what would happen.

Almost every Saturday my husband and I go to a football match, to watch either Aberdeen or Queen of the South –our home in Edinburgh is a great central base. Our two sons have been brought up supporting both teams and regularly attend Aberdeen and Queens matches. Our older son is at Aberdeen University.

This is the story of our Scottish Cup games 2008:

November 2007 and it was off to a freezing cold Peterhead with my husband to see Queens win – great day – so many goals

January 2008 and a trip to Falkirk with our youngest son to see Aberdeen draw – my husband was at Palmerston to see Queens beat Linlithgow Rose. Mid-week I travel to Pittodrie and my oldest son and I see the Dons comfortably beat Falkirk in the replay

February 2008 and a trip to "grotty" Cappielow with my husband to see Queens beat Morton – another great game and we hear Aberdeen scraped past Hamilton (our oldest son was at the game)

Saturday 8th March – a fantastic trip to Palmerston with my husband and youngest son to see Queens beat Dundee – an amazing feeling seeing Queens make it to the semi-final and Ryan McCann's goal!! Driving home we hear the draw for the next round Aberdeen or Celtic v QOS –

Sunday 9th March and I make the trip to Pittodrie and my oldest son and I see Aberdeen almost beat Celtic – must be all over now, but amazingly the Dons win the replay. I would expect that I am unique in that I was the only person to attend both quarter-finals as a passionate supporter of both home teams! Battle lines with my husband were now being drawn up in the house as our two teams were to meet in the semi-final.

Having watched Queens and Aberdeen all season I knew Queens had a good chance of beating Aberdeen if they could play the same team as they did in the quarters v Dundee.

Aberdeen had played inconsistently all season despite a good run in the UEFA Cup and were not good at scoring goals.

However, we knew we would be at the cup final whatever happened, but which team would we be supporting?

The family were divided – after much deliberation, myself and our oldest son Stephen got tickets for the Aberdeen end (as Dons season ticket holders) and my husband and youngest son and friends were at the Queens end.

It is probably the strangest football game I have ever attended as having supported Queens for the last 25 years and all the way to the cup semi-final I could not drum up any hatred for them and could not find my usual passion for the Dons, and by the end Stephen and I were really hoping Queens would hang on as they so deserved it.

Cup final day and it was happy families again as we were all reunited and we had a fantastic day out, despite the result. It was an all blue affair and particularly special for my husband who has supported Queens all his life and attended every game in the 07/08 cup final run. (He was supposed to have been playing an East of Scotland county tennis match in the Isle of Man on 24.05.08 – this was arranged in January and he agreed, never dreaming that Queens would reach the cup final. His fellow players were fantastic, and after the semi-final insisted that he pull out as he couldn't miss a chance of being at Hampden for Queens first ever cup final)

I will continue to support Aberdeen and QOS – my first game for the 2008/09 season (after Aberdeen's friendly against Man Utd), will be at Berwick to see Queens in the Challenge Cup. I just hope that our two teams do not get drawn against each other in the future.

Jennifer Moffat
Edinburgh

The build-up to the Scottish Cup final lasted an eternity and I found sleep difficult to come by in the week leading up to the big match. Did we have a chance against the mighty, but demoralised and tired Rangers? I certainly thought so. There was a real friendly atmosphere at the final, but make no mistake the diehards wanted victory. We didn't turn up in the first half, but what a performance at the start of the second. When Jim Thomson's header blasted into the net, I just remember crazy, wild celebrations everywhere. We may have lost the final, but I was proud to call myself a Doonhamer.

Chris McKie, Bebington, Wirral

I'm a Hearts supporter, Jambo through and through (I even bought my bird a JT nighty!) so how did I find myself at Hampden cheering on QOS against the great unwashed? Because of Hearts' worst season in a long time and I'm nothing but a glory hunter? (possibly), or perhaps I've been subject to indoctrination over the past 10 years. A good pal of mine is a Doonhamer and a lifelong supporter and slowly but surely I've been made to take an interest in this famous old club (only club mentioned in the Bible – yeah yeah, whatever).

The first time I saw Queens in action was at Palmerston on the final day of the 2001/02 season. The Championship had already been won but it was nice to finish with a 4-0 victory anyway. What a really good day it was too, the town bedecked in banners, players stopping in the street for a chat and just a real buzz about the place and a general atmosphere of good humour. Into the "Palmy" afterwards, which was an experience, and then off to paint the town red (or blue) in places like the Globe Howff and the place which has bus seats instead of chairs!!?? The second game was the following season in December, away at Falkirk. Hmm, 5-0 let's say no more! On the plus side I got a Christmas present of a QOS away strip which still graces the Thursday night 5 a sides. The next game was away again, this time in season 2003/04 at Easter Road in the CIS Cup. Another loss unfortunately, 2-1, but it's always good to cheer a goal against that lot! Next was another away trip, this time to Hamilton and the plastic pitch. Memory is failing here but I'm pretty sure it was the Scottish Cup game in January 2006 and yet another defeat (there's a story about abducting a ball boy but best not to go there!).

That brings me bang up to date with my final match (so far!) being that memorable day in Glasgow. Remember when you were a lad and cup final day always seemed to be the sunniest of the year. Well this day didn't disappoint. Into the pub at 11am, a good swally until about 2, a 20 minute meander to the ground exchanging "pleasantries" – they really are a sub-species – and then emerging into a real cracking atmosphere. Abiding memories of the match are obviously the two QOS goals (and we had almost the best seats to see them) and "Wee Bruce" going mental down the front. Afterwards back to the pub again for some post match analysis and a skinful more beer. What a day!

Am I a QOS supporter? No, I suppose not but I don't see anything wrong in wishing them all the best and hoping they do as well as possible – but when they get promoted to the SPL, all bets are off!

Philip Jackson, Edinburgh

A few months ago (mid December) we were 30 minutes away from going bottom of the 1st Division when we were losing at Stirling. Had someone said then that we'd go on a run of 9 wins in a row, hardly lose any more games until the end of the season, finish 4th in the league, score an 84-yard decider in the last minute of the quarter-final, beat Aberdeen 4-3 in the semi including a spell of 5 goals in around 12 minutes, qualify for Europe, have 15,000 supporters going to the final against a Rangers team who had just appeared in the Uefa Cup final and come close to winning 4 trophies, whilst actually believing we were going to beat them, and nearly doing just that after coming back to 2-2 from 2-0 down, we would have laughed our heads off and booked ourselves into the Crichton. Unbelievable!!

We had another great day and were genuinely gutted to lose, but that just shows how far we've come. An estimated 15,000 on the streets and 7,000 at Palmerston gave the team a great reception on the Sunday. Imagine what it would have been like if we'd won. Still our time will come. Roll on next season.

Stuart Rae
Dumfries

Queen of the South were struggling at the bottom of the First Division in January 2007 when Ian McCall announced he had agreed a deal to bring Stevie Tosh, surprisingly told he could go by Gretna following a fall out with Rowan Alexander, to Palmerston. His opening months at the club were ruined by injury but nevertheless he could claim some of the credit for a turnaround in form that led to survival with a game to spare and looked forward to his first full season with the club.

Instead the opening months of 07/08 were a struggle. Asked to play out wide to fill a problem area he always put in a shift but wasn't really able to influence games as he would have liked. It all changed when he was moved to the centre of midfield in that opening cup tie at Peterhead. Able to pull the strings, he was a significant influence in the 5-0 win that followed and we were off and running. Tosh has always been a powerful influence wherever he has been. He's one of football's "characters", always available with a quote for the press, happy to indulge in banter with his own and opposition fans. I first met 'Tosher' when he was a Gretna player and we ended up in the same team at a quiz night. We won, and had a rare old chat about Scottish football into the bargain. Underneath the "rent a quote" persona he's also an intelligent and thinking footballer (though he probably wouldn't thank me for saying it!). When he created a stir with his published views that Junior clubs shouldn't be allowed in the Scottish Cup three days before we met Linlithgow, it maybe wasn't the smartest timing (although it certainly raised the profile of the game)

but it was a genuine thought out view. I don't agree with it but you have to respect the case he put.

The stir caused by his pre-match Linlithgow comments, particularly the throwaway "it's not as if any of them can actually win the cup" line was ironic as the knee-jerk response from many was "it's not as if Queen of the South can either". I doubt many of those people still thought that at 4:10pm on 24th May! Tosh is infectious and ambitious. He drives people on and makes them believe. He said what he did before the Linlithgow game and then went out and ran the game, forcing the own goal that made it 4-0. He was a central figure in the good run that followed. I recall him being interviewed post-match after the 3-2 league win at Dens Park and being asked if Queens could still win the league. "I'm not in the business of giving you guys easy headline quotes", said Tosh with a glint in his eye, before going to do exactly that. "We can only keep winning games and catching the teams in front of us one at a time. It will take a miracle to catch the top two but I'm not ready to give up yet. Some people might be happy to have this club away from the bottom end. Not me. I still want to challenge at the top".

When Morton and Dundee were beaten Tosh became a crucial figure at the club for the semi-final. One of the few to have played, and more especially won, a semi-final before in his Gretna days, and as an ex-Aberdeen player he was a focus for attention both inside and outside the club. He didn't see the game as one last showing on the big stage either. He wanted to win and he believed we would win. He may not be

captain either but he led by example that day. Fifteen minutes in and the ball broke loose outside our box for Severin. He lined up the shot but got nowhere. Stevie Tosh and Jamie McQuilken hared out and literally threw themselves in the path of the ball. It set the tone. Five minutes later when Andy Aitken laid a ball back in the other box no Aberdeen player did the same as Tosh drove us into the lead. The second half was crazy stuff but it was Tosh who played the ball over the top from which O'Connor scored the third and Tosh who picked the team up with the driving run that earned the throw from which the 4th came just after the third equaliser had been lost. And it was Tosh who seemed to spend about three of those four long additional minutes of injury time with the ball at his feet at the corner flag nearest the Queens fans and over 100 yards from our goal. When he earned a free kick with 60 seconds to go in that

corner he turned to the fans thumped his own chest and lifted the roof off the place. This was a man who wasn't prepared to let loose his grip on another Scottish Cup final even at 35 years old. Every bit of the old desire is still there.

The lead up to the final was chaotic down Palmerston way with the attention of the media firmly focused on the club. I covered the office for the week before and I remember 'Tosher' phoning one day to sort something out with his ticket allocation. At the end of the conversation I recall saying to him that I couldn't help but notice I had completely gone without mention in his "Cup Final Diary" in 'The Sun' all week. "Listen big man", said Tosh, "if I named everyone who asked me for a mention they'd have to give me the whole paper." I laughed. It had only been a joke anyway and I certainly didn't expect him to be mentioning me in the national press in cup final week. Nevertheless, on the morning of the final there it was in his column.

The game itself is of course history now. Down and out at half time Tosh gave us hope with one thrust of his hips and did something I never ever thought I'd see. Queen of the South scored in a Scottish Cup final. The final outcome was disappointment all round of course but I spoke to 'Tosher' post-match and told him that at least I'd had a fiver on him to score at any time at 15/2. "That'll be a pint you owe me later then", says he. "Oh, and did you check out the Sun this morning" was added as he disappeared with a wink. I still owe him that pint. Collect it anytime 'Tosher'.

Ewan Lithgow
Dumfries

I was joined at the cup final by friends and members of my family, some of whom had never seen QOS in the flesh, and thought I should give them some information about what to expect. Of particular interest to some of them was why I referred to Jim Thomson as "30-yard Thomson" and I explained that Jim was the team captain, a hero to the fans and an absolute lion in defence – but that every time the ball landed at his feet the inevitable outcome was the ball being punted 30 yards up the pitch, normally ending up out of the ground or in the possession of the opposition. Lack of pressure from an opposition player could not influence this outcome. Indeed, the less the pressure the more inevitable the outcome. I also explained JT's prowess in the air and aggressive tackling and leadership qualities.

During the game Jim did not disappoint with 30 yarders going all over the place. At one point during the second half he even demonstrated his 30 yard ability with his left foot from the left back area, Steven Whittaker of Rangers gratefully accepting the pinpoint pass.

Happily, in the 53rd minute Jim brilliantly gave us living reward from the old adage "do what you are good at", and for all the times I have wondered what goes through his mind before an aimless 30 yard hoof up the pitch I didn't care at that moment as he rose majestically above three Rangers defenders to crash home an unstoppable header and reignite our belief that the cup was going to be ours. What a beautiful goal and what an ecstatic reaction to it from the East Stand at Hampden – watching the replay still sends shivers down my spine.

Occasionally we have been treated to intermittent glimpses of what Jim is capable of, from stunning overhead kick goals to moments of Ronaldinho-esque footwork, but despite this Jim's 30 yard hoof up the pitch remains his speciality.

A Queens game would not be the same for me without a regular helping of "30-yard Thomson". Unlike goals, you know there is one coming up soon. Great stuff Jim, you'll always be a hero to me. And what a goal, thank goodness it was a header!!

Les Morton, Dunblane

When Jim Thomson equalised in the final it was one of the most unbelievable experiences of my life. If that was how we, the supporters felt, how must he have felt when his header flew in??? I met my mate at half-time (I'd gone to the match with my wife, two sons and my maw), and with us two down I commented to him that realism had taken over. Fifteen minutes later, and it was fantasy football time again – we'd got it back to 2-2 and the Rangers players and fans were wilting in front of us. As it was, they bounced back off the ropes and claimed a winner, but I can assure you that, no matter how much a Rangers supporter enjoyed his day, they never experienced a feeling like we all did when JT equalized. We hadn't just made it respectable (I'd have settled for that at half-time), we hadn't even just scored a consolation goal (that's how I felt deep-down when Tosher made it 2-1) we had given Rangers a two-goal start in the Scottish Cup final, and pegged them back to 2-2. That moment will never be bettered for any of us in football-terms.

And so the journey was finished – a much longer than expected journey, which, (and I still can't believe I'm saying this) will now continue, and take Queen of the South into European football next season

Mark McMinn
Dumfries

I came back from France for the Scottish Cup final – in my 23 years as a QOS fan, I knew that such a prestigious opportunity wouldn't happen very often in my lifetime, and whilst I was realistic about our chances of actually winning, I knew I just had to come over – if we won, then I'd regret it for the rest of my life! Luckily we managed to get some tickets through friends in Scotland. Given the rush of sales, that brought a celebration in itself!!

On the day of the final, I was in a group of about 10 folk (including my newly converted-to-QOS girlfriend), and the strange thing was that at least three of them were Rangers fans who were "supporting Queens for the day". It was a really odd thing to do I thought, but in fairness, they had been to the semi too, and when back home, would always try to catch a QOS game. One had actually been in Manchester a few days before. His recollections differed somewhat from the media reports, but did little to alter my perception of Rangers fans, 25,000 of whom were facing us across the park with their Northern Irish flags and jingoistic pseudo-religous songs. The atmosphere was strangely subdued, probably because most of their fans seemed to miraculously turn up 2 minutes before kick-off. There was an element of "they've certainly done this before" about it all. The QOS end was a different prospect altogether, and the atmosphere was genuinely electrifying for a good 25 minutes before kick-off. Except, I was standing with a couple of Rangers fans!

After 15 minutes, I was already thinking the best we can hope for is 0-0 and a penalty shoot-out – we were all over the place, and riding our luck in our own box. I knew it couldn't last. You know when you sometimes get that feeling that a goal is coming? I remember the Rangers forward (Beasley) crumbling on the edge of the box under a brush from Tosh – it really was the softest of decisions and I howled an unintelligable protest and just thought this is it. And it was. It looked like a cracking goal, which sort of took the edge off the decision – somehow it's easier to go behind to really good goals!! Anyway, it changed everything, and QOS suddenly looked vulnerable The second goal was a shambles, and a real killer, timing-wise – 2-0 down against a team who kept out Fiorentina home and away, and we were creating nothing. The dream was over – and the Rangers fans were rubbing it in – "you're

not singing anymore..." they bawled at us. And we weren't either – at least not where I was standing. It was now looking to me like damage limitation – we didn't want to leave Hampden with everyone saying "aye, told you it was a fluke...got what they deserved". We didn't deserve that at all. My mate had smiled at the 2nd Rangers goal, though was completely displeased with the way Rangers were playing. It was a relief that victory seemed assured, and humiliation was going to be avoided.

The second half – how did anyone feel at the start of that? I'm sure I just wanted to call it 2-0 and head off down the pub to toast the "bravehearts" etc – but something was different about both teams from the kick off and QOS immediately came charging down the wing in front of us. It seemed Rangers had come out to bang a few more in, kill the game, and have a party and weren't expecting volume resistance from the "amateurs". When Tosh pelvis-ed the goal that made it 2-1, there was an explosive celebration – just because we had something to celebrate – and I genuinely thought that would be all we would have to celebrate! We've scored against Rangers at Hampden in the cup final – stick it on a t-shirt and a DVD and we'll take that. But things were really happening on the pitch. My Rangers mate's face was now contorted – his arms were itching to gesture anger, but he couldn't give away his true allegiance. Glances were exchanged across the line between the secret Gers fans and in between were the gleeful smiling Doonhamer fans who'd already seen enough to make their day. Then, Jim Thomson rises to make it 2-2 and this is the most surreal moment in football. The Rangers end seem to collectively put their hands over their faces, in one giant movement. The QOS fans are caught between abject euphoria in the good viewing seats and "did that really go in...???" amongst the less well placed fans. Within seconds the sight of Jim Thomson reeling away with a clenched fist and the Rangers defence on their knees in the box confirms that the most unlikely turnaround ever has actually happened. I am delirious bouncing up and down with the rest of the blue and white mass and my Rangers mates are like the 3 pixels that don't work on your TV set – static and chewing the inside of their lips. The roar of "you're not singing anymore" catches fire in

the Queens end and the entire 15,000 fans hurl it back across the stadium. It is momentous, and surely unforgettable. If Queens do this, they will make this film in Hollywood – it will be recalled in hundreds of years and then rebutted as "surely rubbish"!! It's the stuff of myth. And then, the reality began to kick back in – Queens were out on their feet – Rangers cranked it up a notch and started keeping the ball. What happened next is difficult to retell, other than to say, again, I felt it coming. It was going to be a "bravehearts" headline day after all (God, I hate that...), with the plaudits going to the big team – no shocks, just a little hiccup on the way.

As we walked out of Hampden, I felt genuinely elated. We'd lost admirably – not to a fluke, or a penalty shoot-out, or an own goal in the last minute, and certainly not by the type of margin that should separate two sides with such divergent wage bills. There were no "if onlys" for me. But something struck me about the whole atmosphere at Hampden, and indeed in the build-up weeks before. We showed there is dignity and respect in supporting your "ain team" and that it is possible to enjoy football even in defeat. There is no doubt in my mind that my Rangers mates were hugely envious of this – and I suspect a few of the glory-seekers across the stadium had similar thoughts. There was no victory for Rangers at Hampden that day – just another cup, that they were expected to win and would do again next year probably. None of the Rangers players celebrated the goals with any real passion, and the fans responded with equal apathy. The presentation of the cup was one of the biggest anti-climaxes I've ever seen, and while we stood and applauded their team as they accepted their medals, we knew the adventure, the joy, and ultimately, the pleasure, had been all ours. Football can be many things to many people, but its biggest contribution is bringing people together under one banner, to instill a sense of pride in the culture and traditions of a town or city. The jokes and songs are all part of that culture, and when you are one of only a few, your voice seems that wee bit louder. The Scottish Cup final 2008 will long live in the memory of Dumfries folk, for all those reasons. I suspect it has already been forgotten in the west end of Glasgow...

Simon Davidson, Nottingham

Just after 5pm (4pm UK time) Sarah Cullen relaxing on her weekend off near her flat by Lake Como in Italy received the second of three texts from her brother Stuart who was watching TV in a pub in Brighton – it said Queens had equalised the score was 2-2. Unfortunately the first and third texts gave the half time and full time scores. Stuart then tried to phone his brother Andrew who was at Hampden with me (their Dad) but with no luck as Andrew was texting his girlfriend Lisa in Sligo, Eire with the same news. Andrew and I had met up in Dublin where he works and flown to Prestwick the night before travelling to the match with the Sanquhar branch of the QOS supporters club. Around the same time Maggie Cullen (whose only interest in football had emerged during the second half of the Aberdeen match!) texted her son Andrew from our home in SW France saying " what a comeback – hope they win!" Andrew's Uncle Ian was doubly overjoyed, not only had Queens equalised but the other viewers in the bar in Basingstoke had been about to change channel to the Wembley playoffs but suddenly they had become Queens supporters!!

All these facts are true, let me explain…

Although I left Sanquhar in 1958 and all my seven children were born in the London area, the first football club they ever heard of was Queen of the South.

From the first match after the war against Hibs in August 1945 until 1958, boarding school apart, I didn't miss many matches at Palmerston. Although Billy Houliston was my hero, my greatest memories are of the 1950 semi-final (Roy Henderson and Dougie Sharpe's mix-up cancelling out Jackie Brown's great goal) and season 1954-55 when we topped the table until Ne'erday. I remember a special train to Paisley on New Year's Day, Willie Telfer's two goals in the last minutes making it 5-3 for St Mirren. The next day we lost 6-2 at home to Partick Thistle (Jackie McGill broke his leg) and the dream was over! The team is embedded in my mind.

Drummond Cullen, St Savinien, France

Rangers and St Johnstone took a bit of time sorting out who would play Queens. We spent the time trying to work out what was the better option – if we played Rangers it would be a bigger occasion and we'd be in the UEFA Cup! But if it was St Johnstone -could we win it? But if St Johnstone beat us then we'd have nothing. St Johnstone did really well but it was to be Rangers. More ticket panic, but enough season ticket holders and share-holders between us for everyone to get a ticket- even my wife. Whole families turned up – I've never seen so many little old ladies at a football game! Pal Stevie (who missed all the goals in the semi in the pie queue) turns up with his face painted. Unfortunately he did it himself in the mirror so its back to front and he has something like 2OQ written on both cheeks. He eventually wipes it off as strangers keep pointing and laughing at him. We have dozens of balloons, sombreros, inflatables etc for the party atmosphere. Queens fans all over the south side of Glasgow. Like going to a Scotland game. Hope this isn't the last time I experience that! My mate Big Al (a serial gambler) is envious my ante-post bet on Queens has got me about £650 even if we get beaten. That will pay for the Euro trip at least! Big Al is so nervous he can't drink his pre-match pint – I can relate to that, definite pre-match nerves for me too!

Nacho Novo is suspended for the final, but worryingly that lets in big match specialist Kris Boyd who duly thunders one past Jamie in the first half that is more or less unstoppable. 1-0 down although we were holding our own until then. Still we know from the semi that we can score against SPL teams so the heads are not down yet. Then a couple of uncharacteristic errors in defence let in Beasley to score a soft second 2-0. Fans a bit low, but still singing. Second half and a different Queens come out. Big Sean and Tosh combine to score a good if unorthodox reply 2-1. Seconds later it seems and Bob Harris sends a pinpoint free kick over for JT to thunder home a headed equaliser! 2-2. For the next short while we are on top and the adrenalin is going. Then Boyd again gets his head on a cross and its 3-2 Rangers. Although we were never out of it, in truth we probably needed to keep it at 2-2 and hope for extra time and penalties. A few of us had a tear in the eye at the end when the lads did their lap of honour.

Head out for a few beers in Glasgow after the game and to be fair, any Rangers fans we met were complimentary about Queens – hope they are as magnanimous when we beat them next time! Accosted by a couple of overweight 50-something "ladies" with identikit peroxide hair, in McGinns Bar under Central Station. Looking appraisingly at our kilts one asks if we are true Scotsmen – we respond as to whether they are true blondes – one cackles so hard her false teeth fall into her Lambrusco and we make a lucky escape before either question is put to the test.....

Andy Paterson
Houston, Renfrewshire

We had been waiting excitedly for some time. The DVD player was on burn out mode as we viewed the semi-final win over Aberdeen for the umpteenth time. For me it was a late night necessity, Balvennie in hand. For my two boys, a regular 8 o'clock supplement for their Coco-Pops.

We were ready for this!

Saturday morning arrived, and we decided to sit and watch the highlights of all media coverage over the past week. It had been a frenzy at every Queens training session so we sat and savoured every interview, player profile and of course, every pun on the name Queen of the South. I explained to the boys, this was not as it always was; scouring the tabloids every day as a teenager to find even one column inch on the team. They looked at me in disbelief.

This was Queens first cup final and hey, did we know it! I began to feel a degree of responsibility. I had introduced them to this team and felt it would be me that would burden any responsibility should Queens be humiliated. My wife is from Glasgow and the two boys grew up in Gourock. They had assumed pretty well an affiliation with the club if even in a "distant learning" fashion. They have, however, accepted the role readily and are bordering on the obsessed. Our collective emotions had been focused on this event for a number of weeks. The long lay off between the last league game and the final itself, had only increased the excitement to intolerable measures. We had kicked every ball in the semis and felt a shared expectation with each and every player.

We headed to Glasgow, stopping off at the Ferry for refreshments. On arrival in the city it seemed that every taxi driver peeped their horn at our car which we had draped in Queens colours. We could tell that this was no ordinary cup final. Having followed Scotland's journey through the Euro 2008 qualifiers I had hoped that in some way, the atmosphere could be recreated as we headed towards Hampden.

As we neared the ground, we were greeted by thousands of fans as well as film cameras eager to capture the build up. The flags were being waved, familiar songs sung and the sea of Queens blue and white shirts before me helped to ensure that my earlier expectations were not only met but exceeded. Mardi Gras had come to Hampden and Queens fans were providing the party. We had rehearsed the songs and re-rehearsed the songs over and over. Inside the ground, the supporters belted them out in unison. I had excited nods of approval from the family. They were impressed! Their faces shone with excitement. This was their moment. This was my moment. This was our family's moment.

The game started and nerves took over. As I surveyed the huge support, I saw many sharing my apprehension. Our nerves worsened. By half time we were 2 nil down. We had endured tremendous pressure. I knew we could do better. The second half blasted us away instantly. No sooner had we finished singing the Railway Line and Queens had scored 2 goals to make it 2-2. Our support, more relaxed, sang. And boy did they sing! Drowning out Rangers fans with ease. We became a voice, a machine of unity and a group determination evolved which we knew had never been witnessed in the club's 89-year history. As we continued to grow momentum, a blow. Rangers scored what proved to be the winning goal.

I cried. Others were equally emotional. Their grief apparent. We tried again for an equaliser but it was not to be.

My boys had grown in such affection towards this club and had experienced such fluctuations of mood during the game, but overall they had a huge amount of pride and joy at the way in which we had played. I could tell that the love for this club would be a lifelong family affair. No question. Our decision to head to Dumfries for the night only served to remind us how altogether magnificent the achievement had been. We partied into the wee small hours with friends and acquaintancies met through the years of support.

The day will live with us forever, and we can only hope that our family (which now includes another 15,000 others) can enjoy just a fraction of this emotion again!

Murray Sutherland
Gourock

The last few minutes at Hampden in the semi-final urging the referee to blow his whistle, then my fiancée seeing me cry for the first time!

Not being able to get a ticket for the final and a desperate search that ended with me driving from Blackpool to Gretna one afternoon to meet a guy I didn't know at the Gateway shopping village to get a couple of tickets off him.

The games themselves covering a whole range of emotions that I don't think I will ever go through again.

And finally the comment that will always stick in my mind is, whilst walking back to the car after the final and my other half said" We should remember our way in for the next time we are here" I just loved her optimism

Simon Jowitt

Norcross

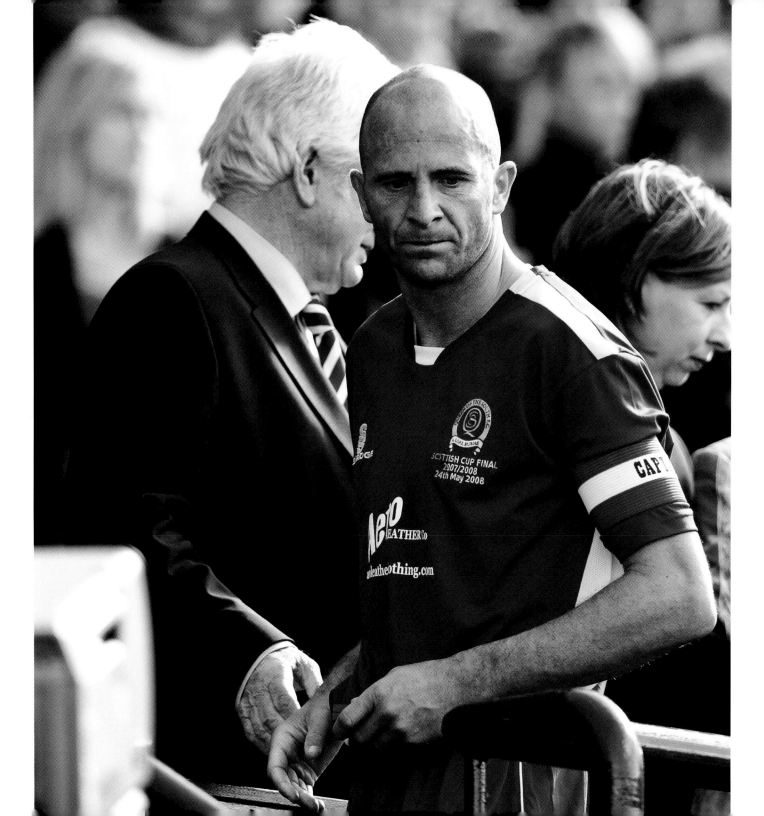

CHAPTER 7
THE PRIDE OF DUMFRIES

Every now and then a team from a lower league emerges to make their mark in the Scottish Cup and this past season it has been Queen of the South. Our journey commenced in the snows of Peterhead in November and culminated in the sunshine of the national stadium some six months later.

En-route we faced Junior side Linlithgow Rose who were 'breaking new ground' by just playing in the competition, knocked out Morton at their own Cappielow before beating Dundee with an epic never-to-be-forgotten 84-yard clincher. In our first four ties we netted 13 goals without reply – a feat in itself, but all that changed in a seven-goal semi-final thriller at Hampden which we edged 4-3.

We did fall at the final hurdle, losing 3-2 to Rangers but it was a 'glorious failure' and a match which our generation of fans will never forget. 86,370 spectators witnessed those six cup-ties with our own support totaling 32,642. So now it's on to Europe!

Bill Goldie
Queen of the South FC

After the heroics by the team in getting to the Scottish Cup final, a great turn out the next day to cheer the boys home was more than deserved. I must admit I was a bit apprehensive with Queens not lifting the cup that the town would not show up in great numbers to support the boys on their homecoming.

HOW WRONG WAS I???

The bus set off from the DG1 Centre where there were crowds of people lining both sides of the streets. By the time it reached the bottom of the High Street the place seemed to be mobbed with well wishers and the atmosphere was electric to say the very least. I would say it felt like the whole of the townspeople and most probably visitors to the town were out in force to show the boys just how very proud we all were of their achievement in getting into the final.

Once the bus left the High Street it came down Buccleuch Street and over the bridge making its way to Palmerston. One of my most favourite memories of the whole cup experience is looking back when I was just going over the bridge and seeing a sea of people with their blue and white flags and scarves flying with pride. I am sure it would have brought a tear to many a fan's eye.

Once the bus reached Palmerston Park the players were cheered on to the pitch one by one by about 6,000 fans so proud to welcome Queens home. The biggest cheer I would have to say went out to our chairman David Rae, (what a character!) who has ploughed (no pun intended!) thousands of pounds of his hard earned money and years of his time into a club he truly loves.

Iain Wright
Dumfries

They gave us all we could ask for, took us somewhere few of us ever dreamt of going, and will be remembered by Queens fans forever – thank you to them all.

Mark McMinn
Dumfries

Having enjoyed the Friday and Saturday of cup final weekend, there was more to come on the Sunday with the open-top bus parade through Dumfries. This event proved to me how much the success of the club meant to the town in general. My son was too young for the trip to Hampden but joined me in the parade following the bus along the High Street, Buccleuch Street, Glasgow Road and into Palmerston for a celebratory event that I could only compare with that day back in April 2002 when a packed Palmerston Park witnessed the trophy presentation to the Second Division champions following a 4-0 demolition of Morton. Later that day my son asked, "Can I come to the final next year Dad?" – here's hoping!

How can next season possibly compete with events in 2008 so far? No need to worry on that score as the Queen of the South European tour kicks off in August.

Up the Queens!

Gordon Harper, Dumfries

For the last game of 2007/08, at the end of what the owner of a rival First Division club described as "a miracle season", Queens took almost 16,000 people to Hampden to cheer them on in the club's first ever Scottish Cup final. What a fantastic turnout with people coming back from all over the world to support the team on an historic occasion. Demand exceeded supply and even more tickets could have been sold if we could have obtained them.

If you get the chance only once in your life to do something you want to do take it, because if you don't you can never do it again. We may hope that another opportunity presents itself but history would suggest that this was a once in a lifetime occasion.

The crowds on the streets of Dumfries and at Palmerston for the "Parade" the day after the final were estimated at between 5,000 and 8,000 and the town and the stadium were a sea of blue and white. What a fantastic sight this was as the sun shone brightly on the celebrations.

So far was this from a freezing April night in Livingston just a few weeks earlier, when a mere 96 Queens fans saw a 1-0 defeat, that it's incredible so many turned out for the final. Now I know we can't compare these 2 games and, lets face it, away to Livingston on a freezing Tuesday night is for the absolute diehards only ("hello" to the other 95 diehards by the way) but the only way the club is going to keep going upwards is if crowds at Palmerston get bigger. Our 4th place finish in the league in 2007/08 is historically, with a few exceptions, as good as it gets and it was a fantastic season with more highs than lows. But the average home attendance for league games was less than 2,000.

When Palmerston is full – Hibs QF in 2006/07 (lost 2-1), Dundee QF in 2007/08 (won 2-0) – the atmosphere is brilliant and the occasions fantastic. The camaraderie evident at these events is one of the great joys of life.

When it's not full -1,702 at the Partick Thistle game a few days after the semi-final v Aberdeen – things are not so good even if we are winning. Big crowds make a huge difference to the players, to the club's finances and to the other fans. There is no question the club has tremendous potential – we could really become an established SPL team – but this potential will never be realized unless more people come to the games. I truly believe that Queens fans are as good as any and better than most, the problem is there's not enough of us (cup semis and finals excepted) turning up regularly to support the team and the club.

There may be many good and valid reasons for this and it is sometimes not easy being a Queens fan, but, if even half the people in Dumfries who are interested in the Queens result at 5 o'clock on a Saturday evening went along to the games Palmerston would be packed for every game.

I sincerely hope the legacy of the 2007/08 cup campaign will be a renewed interest in the club and an upsurge in attendances at Palmerston.

On 24th May the players, management and chairman all did us proud in delivering a (so far) once in a lifetime experience. How we all appreciated them on that day. Let more of us appreciate them on a more regular basis and you never know where it will lead.

C'mon the South

Yer Hame Team's Yer Ain Team

Les Morton

Dunblane

On the Sunday after the final we decided to go direct to Palmy rather that wait for the bus as we thought we would get a better view – we were right. Took up a positon right next to the dug out and got my cup final strip signed by the players – at one point I was in the tunnel chatting to Doddsy, John O'Neill and Chis. What a turn-out that day – I don't think that there would have been anymore there if we had won the cup. Fiona then got her photo taken with Dobbs.

We left Dumfries to head back to the Blue Toon and when we were on the M8 – heading for Ikea to get a frame for my strip – John O'Neill and Neil Scally spotted our car – it still had some streamers on it from the day before along with our scarves and some posters – both of them were almost hanging out of their car giving us big waves and huge smiles – a perfect end to a perfect day.

The whole weekend was totally unbelievable – it will stay with us for ever.

Derek and Fiona Kirkpatrick, Peterhead

Queens' Scottish Cup run was nothing short of phenomenal. Despite following the Brown family tradition of supporting the Doonhamers from childhood, never in my wildest dreams on the long journey to Peterhead did I think we'd make it to Hampden. What an experience, what an achievement, another piece of Queens' history. I always have been and always will be proud to be a Queen of the South fan.

Sandra Brown, BBC Sport Scotland

The amazing scenes during the parade made me wonder what on earth Dumfries would have been like had we actually won the cup final. I don't think we would have managed to fit everyone into Palmerston. It was great to see and speak with the players on that special day; that's what supporting a community-based football club is all about.

I feel privileged to have witnessed some of the proudest moments in the history of Queen of the South. Thank you to all the players, staff and directors who made it all possible. I must finish with a special mention to Davie Rae, a man who exclaimed that "Queen of the South is my life." I know exactly how he feels.

Chris McKie, Bebington, Wirral

Seven years ago, my father and I went to see a new Robert Duvall movie called A Shot at Glory, which was about a fictional soccer team, Kilnockie, as they struggled to reach their first Scottish Cup final. It was a forgettable film and, in an unjust world, we dismissed the inevitable happy ending as improbable fiction.

But truth, it turns out, is equally implausible as my home town club, Queen of the South, made it to the Scottish Cup final for the first time in their 89-year history to face the mighty Rangers.

Emerging from the wilderness years (1919-2008) has prompted a bewildering range of emotions about the central role these perennial long shots have played in my life, particularly in my relationship with my father, who passed away last August. Legendary Scottish coach Bill Shankly (on whom Mr. Duvall's character was modelled) was once quoted as saying: "Some people think football is a matter of life and death. I don't like that attitude. I can assure them it is much more serious than that."

For Shanks this was a truism -- he was once outraged at having been accused of taking his wife to see an unglamorous Lancashire side, Rochdale, for their anniversary. "Of course, not. It was her birthday. Would I have got married in the football season? Anyway, it was Rochdale reserves," he grouched.

In some respects this was true of my father, a man who took his future wife to a minor English soccer match on their second date, the first having been to a wrestling bout.

But for me, there have been periods of disenchantment during the progression from childhood to fatherhood. I was

first taken to Palmerston Park to watch Queens in the early 1970s by my father, when they'd fallen on particularly hard times. Cold, wet, windy afternoons were warmed only by cups of steaming Bovril (a biohazard-like beef drink), while "Chopper" Dickson maimed his opponents before hoofing the ball out of the ground. Still, much like Monty Python's Four Yorkshiremen, who were so poor they drank out of rolled up newspaper, we were happy in those days.

I loved Queens so much, they loved me back. They made me a ball boy, responsible for retrieving the errant shots of hackers like Chopper. We were permitted into the locker room to sweep up the mud from their boots and clean the scum from the giant bath that looked like its water supply came direct from the River Ganges. We even got paid -- 15 pence and a Scotch pie.

In 1979-1980, Queens placed bottom but one of the entire Scottish football ladder and it was suddenly uncool to support the Doonhamers. One urban legend has it that a disillusioned

announcer even introduced the crowd to the players, so few were the numbers in attendance. At the age of 13, I fell out of love with Queens -- and, coincidentally, round about the same time I tried cigarettes, alcohol and civil disobedience at home.

My father and I grew close again the moment I left home for university, and closer still when my demands on his net income ended. But Queens and I never reconciled. They were still my "hame team" but I was living in Glasgow and watching Celtic and Rangers play Europe's elite. I had traded up from my provincial roots.

Then 10 years ago, I moved to Canada and Queens once again assumed a pivotal role in my life. My mid-day phone calls with my Dad every Saturday became an institution--a post-mortem on the Queens' game and a 15-minute discussion on the latest football flotsam would be concluded with off-hand inquiry into my mother's welfare. Maybe it was because we didn't have much else to talk about but it was a point of real connection that I still miss acutely.

These exchanges were even responsible for encouraging my father into cyberspace at a time when he couldn't even use a bank auto-teller. Queens were playing an important cup game and I checked the live score online to discover they were leading. I phoned home at half-time and was greeted with a scoff of disbelief. "I'd have heard the roar," said the old man, possible given we could see the Palmerston flood-lights from our house. The next day, my mother called to say he'd just had thousands of pounds of computer equipment installed.

I'm left to conclude he was something of a jinx on the Queens. He passed away last August and they have been virtually unbeatable ever since. When they won the quarter-final game I found his e-mail address on my Black-Berry -- I've been unable to delete it -- and sent him a note to let him know we made it. I think he got it -- at any rate, it didn't bounce back as undeliverable.

Maybe it's just as well he wasn't around to watch the semi-final against Aberdeen last Saturday. He had a notoriously nervous stomach and this was a white knuckle ride. Three times Queens led against their more illustrious opponents, three times Aberdeen equalized. Then, with half an hour to go, Queens scored a fourth and Aberdeen had nothing left to give.

My six-year-old son James accompanied me to the final — both wearing our Queens' colours with pride, just as I did half-a-lifetime ago when I first went to see them with my own Dad. It's only a game but as every football fan knows, in many ways, it's much more important than that.

John Ivison, Ottawa, Canada

On Sunday 27th January, 1974 my father took me to my first ever match at Palmerston – a Scottish Cup third round tie against East Fife which Queens won 1-0 in front of a crowd of 5,400. Aged six at the time, I must have enjoyed the experience as it started a life long obsession with Queen of the South.

Thirty four years later, I did something I never dreamt possible and took my own son, Finlay, aged four, to his first Scottish Cup tie – the 2008 Scottish Cup final against Rangers at Hampden Park in front of a crowd of more than 48,000. I hope it's not the last time either of us experience this great occasion but what a way to start your football journey!

Craig Paterson
Director, Queen of the South FC

WELL DONE QUEENS

I followed the cup run on Footymad and BBC texts, here in Santa Monica, California. When Queens reached the final I knew had to be there. I'd followed them all my life and growing up in Lincluden I used to walk to Palmerston. Around five years ago, I bought a few shares to help the club and was delighted to discover I had priority on tickets and got five.

My youngest son David lives in Dumfries and he and I went to the final on a bus from the Baker Street pub. It had a great carnival atmosphere and good crack with everyone enjoying themselves. We met my other son Chris, his father-in-law Andy and brother-in-law Kevin, who lives in Falkirk, at the Montford near Hampden. At sixty years of age, I never thought I would see this day and thank God I did. It was brilliant, particularly the atmosphere at the game itself. Although disappointed to lose, the result seemed secondary. I watched Scotland in the old days with 134,000 fans creating an electric atmosphere but when Jim Thomson's equaliser went in I can honestly say the elation I felt was better than anything I had ever experienced previously – the noise was deafening and the moment itself simply unforgettable.

The entire weekend was unbelievable and I had to choke back tears on many occasions in particular when a guy in The Globe started playing the bagpipes following our return from Hampden. Then, just after the goosepimples had disappeared, the parade arrived and I could not have been more proud of the team as thousands lined the streets to pay tribute and say thanks to all involved in this fairy tale. I managed to get my St Andrew's Cross flag with QOS Santa Monica on it signed by most of the players including the two goalscorers and Gordon Chisholm. It now hangs proudly back in my bedroom in California. Thanks for the memories.

John Rodgers
Santa Monica, California

What an amazing Scottish Cup journey, from beginning to end I loved every minute of it! I have supported Queens since I was eleven years old, my first game was a nil-nil draw with Brechin at Palmerston and I still came back! That's because there is something really special about Queens, I know every supporter of every other club thinks that, but in this case it really is true.

I have always said to people Queens would do something very special, even the Champions League! Nobody ever believed me and laughed at me! Now we are heading to the UEFA Cup!

I hope Davie Rae liked my Queens hat! I planted it on him at the end of the Dundee game, my Dad got it made for me in Texas of all places! He has to go back and get me another one now! I think Queens have been really lucky with their last three Chairmen. All have moved them on and done something special.

All of the team, manager, coaches and chairman have been outstanding. For me though, Jim Thomson has epitomised the spirit of Queen of the South, not only this cup season but throughout his time at Queens.

I don't know how any of the players managed to keep their nerve in any of the cup games, I was shaking and feeling sick, especially at the end of the Aberdeen game. Congratulations and thanks to them all, memories I will never, ever forget.

Robert Richardson
Dalbeattie

At Christmas 2007 we took my daughters, aged 25 and 20, along to the club shop with the intention of getting them each a Queen of the South tartan scarf – fashionable and trendy enough for them without being brazenly football scarves. Not surprisingly the shop was closed. However, we rang the front doorbell and who should answer the bell but David Rae himself. The chairman recognized me from a previous encounter and, much to our surprise, he invited us in and gave us a tour of the premises.

As we stood on the hallowed turf David was charming and full of stories. My girls looked bewildered as I explained to them that this had been my "field of dreams" as a teenager, since they find it hard to understand what anybody actually did before videos, DVD's, mobile phones, PC's and the internet were invented. To have had a mere two TV channels is simply beyond their comprehension.

Standing on the pitch with two "old" men reminiscing about glorious days far in the past solicited body language of patience and tolerance – well maybe it was pity! David was in his element and his pride in the club was truly something to behold. If ever I thought I was passionate about QOS (which is not in doubt) this was a different league and it was humbling to listen to a man who has done so much for the club but who has no "airs and graces" about him.

To say that what happened in the next 6 months was unexpected would be the understatement of the century. That David Rae would achieve national recognition, that the hair and the yellow anorak would become famous, that he would proudly and memorably represent what it means to be a QOS fan to the national (and international) media – well, you couldn't make it up, could you? But it couldn't have happened to a nicer man.

Genuine, devoted, humble and generous, a man of the people – this is the kind of man every football club wants as the leader. Queen of the South must be one of the most fortunate teams in Scottish football to have as chairman someone whose only aim is to give success to the club, the supporters and the town. His personal investment has kept the club solvent in recent years and it is unbelievably fitting that he should be rewarded in the most glorious way, a first ever cup final appearance. David has achieved success by standing by his principles, not by being flashy, always remembering that the club's future has to be protected. He has led the club to the greatest success in its history and has delivered (along with others) a time that will never be forgotten. What a legacy!

As we left Palmerston that day I said to the girls, "If you turn up at Celtic Park or Ibrox and ring the doorbell I bet the chairman doesn't answer the door, invite you in and give you a tour of the stadium". Wearing their Queens tartan scarves at the cup final they certainly recognized one of the QOS party – they instantly recognized the great man himself.

David Rae, Chairman of Queen of the South, you are the man – you truly are the King of Queens.

Les Morton, Dunblane

The New Bazaar Doonhamers held their annual "SQA" exam after the last game of the season. As is usual, players, backroom staff and board members pop in for a while on their way to the Travel Club dance.

Chairman Rae stopped by and stayed for a long time chatting to many people.

He took some time to chat to me and Callum Grierson.

Among other things we discussed how the town was buzzing with the prospect of our first Scottish Cup final.

David told us that he had been chatting with the hairdressers in a local salon that morning when he went in for a haircut.

I remember the look on Callum's face which reflected my thoughts: "You've had a haircut today??"

Robbie Purdie
Dumfries

I don't care what tradition dictates. When I get married, I want Davie Rae to give me away.

Harley Freemantle
Dumfries Courier

Absent Friens
(Fur A' Queens Fans Depairted)

Nae langer wi' us
Ye cuidnae see
Whit the team wis daein;
Nae tear wis in yir ee,
Nae smile on yir face
Under the clay,
Ye cuidnae savour
The impossibility
O' the langest-ever goal,
The defeat o' the Dons –
Whae cuid've imagined
Gemmes like yon?
Maybe frae a clood
Ye've been luikin doon,
Seen the goals gaan in,
Shared the hopes o the toon –
Delirium, delight,
The place in a haze
O' emotion unkent
In yir livin' days.
Ah'd like tae believe it;
It disnae seem fair
That the team did well
And ye wernae there.
Donald Adamson, Dalbeattie